"*It Starts with Clients* is an impressive greatest hits compendium, distilling Andrew's many years of experience and powerful insights into one highly readable volume. Whether you are new to his material or refreshing your knowledge, by following these eminently practical recommendations you will build better relationships whatever the stage of your career."

—Myles Corson, Markets Leader, Financial Accounting Advisory Services, Ernst & Young

"I love this book. What sets it apart from imitators is the way Andrew Sobel combines decades of experience with fresh new perspectives to give us actionable insights. *It Starts with Clients* delivers the definitive success formula for winning and keeping clients."

—Dave Bencivengo, President, Weichert Workforce Mobility

"A treasure trove of practical advice based on deep experience and research. Andrew Sobel provides a powerful roadmap for relationship building that I have seen both new and experienced people learn from and translate into real results. Sobel's insights are as relevant to the social sector as they are to business. I highly recommend it."

—Jeff Bradach, Managing Partner and Co-Founder, The Bridgespan Group

"Our business begins and ends with clients, and Andrew Sobel's *It Starts with Clients* builds on his earlier works—*All for One* and *Power Questions*—by providing the reader with a roadmap for building and sustaining long-term client relationships. Andrew's practical, hands-on experience with clients across the globe gives him a unique perspective that allows him to stand out as a coach extraordinaire. *It Starts with Clients* is a solid framework for success, I recommend it for everyone who is looking to develop clients for life!"

—Michael Guralnik, Managing Director, Citibank, and Global Head of Marketing, Intellectual Capital Management, and Digital Client Advisory, Treasury and Trade Solutions

"Andrew Sobel is truly a global expert on building client relationships. He focuses on bringing value to *every* relationship. In this latest work, Andrew breaks down the complex issues of building client relationships into a step-by-step action plan that is both easy to understand and follow. Well done!"

—Karen Greenbaum, President and CEO, Association of Executive Search and Leadership Consultants (AESC)

"When looking for sound, practical advice that actually works in building client relationships, I've never found better than Andrew Sobel's wisdom. His mentorship and expertise are laid out in meaningful and actionable approaches in this latest stroke of genius."

—Colin Dominish, Global Market Development Leader, GHD Digital

"This is a comprehensive, practical guide for every professional who wants to succeed at consultative sales and grow their client base. *It Starts with Clients* provides a systematic and programmatic approach, rich with detailed, how-to strategies for winning new clients and earning their long-term loyalty."

—Nagaraja Srivatsan, Chief Digital Officer for R&D Solutions, IQVIA

"In *It Starts with Clients*, Andrew Sobel has given us a powerful how-to guide for the next generation of client advisory professionals—but it's *so much more* than that. Sculpted from a mountain of experience, it is as inspiring as it is instructive; and as easy to read as it is to put into action."

—Adam Reeder, Partner and Global Building Products Co-Head, Rothschild & Co.

"Many of us have benefited from the lessons in Andrew's bestsellers. *It Starts with Clients* sets out an entirely practical and wholly digestible 100-day plan which, while especially useful for younger professionals, has relevance for all of us as advisors. I highly recommend this book, with its anecdotes and their powerful messages—and the novel illustrations."

—Sir Win Bischoff, Chairman, JP Morgan Securities, plc

"*It Starts with Clients* just reaffirms how much I appreciate and value Andrew Sobel's unique perspective on how to build strong relationships. The roadmap he lays out is authoritative, practical, and actionable, making this a must-read that will dramatically accelerate the growth of your clients and your business."

—Nichole Jordan, National Managing Partner, Growth and Performance, Grant Thornton

"This book is tremendous! Based on decades of experience, renowned client relationship expert Andrew Sobel shows us why he is such a respected thought leader in this field. His powerful wisdom, strategies, and practical 'how-to's' on building client relationships are priceless. This kind of advice is rare. I highly recommend it!"

—Stephen M. R. Covey, *New York Times* and #1 *Wall Street Journal* bestselling author of *The Speed of Trust* and *Smart Trust*

"A very powerful, concise, must-read guide for any professional who is seeking to build lifelong, profitable client relationships. Andrew has thoroughly mastered the knack of sharing great lessons in a wonderfully easy and enjoyable read!"

—Diana Brightmore-Armour, CEO, UK and EMEA, ANZ Bank

"Andrew Sobel's ideas are a master class on how to build client relationships with senior decision-makers. *It Starts with Clients* should be required reading for anyone whose career success depends on them."

—Stuart Jackson, Global Managing Partner, L.E.K. Consulting

"Andrew takes the big principles for building strong client relationships and boils them down into clear, practical steps that achieve big results. I also love the 100-day approach, which adds urgency to these important challenges. A great read."

—Michael Hertz, Chief Marketing Officer, White & Case

# IT STARTS WITH CLIENTS

ANDREW SOBEL

# IT STARTS WITH CLIENTS

## YOUR 100-DAY PLAN TO BUILD LIFELONG RELATIONSHIPS AND REVENUE

WILEY

Published by John Wiley & Sons, Inc., Hoboken, New Jersey.

Published simultaneously in Canada.



***Library of Congress Cataloging-in-Publication Data:***

ISBN 9781119619109 (Hardcover)
ISBN 9781119619123 (ePDF)
ISBN 9781119619116 (ePub)

Cover design: Wiley
Cover image: © Gaurav Paswan/Shutterstock

Chapter illustrations by Elizabeth Cupich
Graphics by Lauren Ball

Printed in the United States of America
V10017480_021320

*To the great relationships in my life, starting with my extraordinary wife, Mary Jane; my children Chris, Elizabeth, and Emma; and my friends and clients. And to the late Jerry Panas, my co-author and dear friend, who inspired me to see the cup as always completely full.*

# Contents

# Day 1 The Star of Your Show

On the third day at my new job, something stopped me dead in my tracks. It happened as I walked to the coffee machine.

I stood in the hallway outside of Scott Cunningham's office, entranced. Staring through the half-open door, I watched Scott take a phone call from the CEO of one of the firm's best clients. His feet were up on his desk, bathed by the morning light from his window. He was like a confident jungle cat, basking in the sun. For Scott, work wasn't just interesting—it was downright fun.

I had just finished business school, and that August I began work for a leading management consulting firm in Boston. Scott was a senior partner and former Harvard Business School professor. Still in his 40s, he had big bushy eyebrows and an absurdly thick head of unruly, dark hair. He oozed relaxation. As he spoke on the phone, he periodically crumpled up used Post-it Notes and pitched them into his waste can.

Why was I so taken by this scene? Because Scott was a supreme rainmaker. He had been instrumental in growing the firm from its early days. He knew lots of CEOs and other top executives, and they frequently called him for advice. When Scott wrote proposals, the project was already sold—the proposal was just a memorandum of what he had already agreed upon with the client. No competitive bids, no torturous "Requests for Proposal" (RFPs) to endure.

Scott's office was a nexus of important people who wanted to hire him and our firm. No wonder, as he had an uncanny ability to quickly grasp clients' key issues and conjure up an incisive, original strategy for them. Once a project was sold, he then marshaled other consultants to help deliver the work. These included young associates, like me, as well as other partners who—sadly—just could not attract enough of their own clients.

I immediately knew I wanted to be like Scott, not one of those partners who was consigned to execute what Scott sold. I coveted his mojo. I recognized I had to first learn the business and become a skilled consultant. But I never took my eye off that picture of Scott: thrown back in his chair, fielding important calls, and shooting little yellow basketballs as he gave sage advice to powerful businesspeople.

## This is your playbook

I became a student of Scott's playbook with clients, and carefully watched others like him. I made a lot of mistakes, for sure. But by intentionally putting what I learned to work, I became the youngest partner in our firm at age 31. By 36 I was a senior vice president and country chief executive officer. Then, I started my own successful management consulting company, and embarked on over 20 years of proprietary research to codify the strategies, skills, and techniques that enable you to consistently succeed with clients. Along the way, I've published nine books on developing enduring client relationships, including the international bestsellers *Power Questions* and *Clients for Life*.

In building your own client or customer base, you will invariably face a series of difficult challenges. Many professionals get discouraged and even broken by them. I've selected the 14 most important ones, and I'm going to share with you exactly how to overcome and master each of them. As we go through them, you'll learn proven strategies to consistently develop, grow, sustain, and multiply your client relationships. I've worked with over 50,000 professionals around the world who have successfully used these very same techniques. Put them to work yourself, and they will have a dramatic impact on your success.

If you apply the ideas from each week of this 100-day program, no matter where you are starting from today, you'll grow your client base and revenues. You'll also be in huge demand as a "bankable star" who can reliably start up, grow, or resuscitate any kind of business. You will be *indispensable*. A rainmaker.

Remember, however, that the real star of this movie is your *client*, as shown in the illustration at the beginning of this chapter. You become a bankable star only because you've put your clients in the footlights on center stage, and helped them succeed. As soon as you start making it all about you, and how clever *you* are, people will whisper behind your back. And what they say won't be pretty.

## It starts with clients

Whether you're in the early stage of your career, starting your own business, or are already an experienced practitioner who wants to work more at the C-suite level, this book will save you years of time.

In 100 days you will develop a plan and sharpen your skills to build lifelong relationships and revenue. The core content consists of 14 weeks, one challenge per week. If you spend a day on the introduction and conclusion, and a week on each of the 14 challenges, this adds up to 100 days of reading, analyzing, planning—and acting. Regardless of your level of experience, I am certain you will discover meaningful opportunities to grow your business.

Each week can be read on its own, so feel free to gravitate to those sections most relevant to your particular development needs. As the book progresses, the challenges become more advanced.

### The bar is now much higher

Simply put, selling to and serving clients, especially large corporate clients, is a challenging business. It requires a higher level of skill and business acumen than it used to. Clients are growing increasingly more sophisticated and demanding. So no matter how good you are today, tomorrow you will have to be just a little bit better to get the same results.

## The mindset shift that yields remarkable results

Your expertise and domain knowledge are essential to your success with clients. They are your ticket to entry. They help you add value in the very first conversation with a prospective client. And they often earn you the right to a second meeting. If your clients perceive you can help them, then they will be drawn toward a relationship with you.

*However* . . . an excessive "expert" or "product" focus can get you into trouble. For example, a very successful firm asked me to coach one of their executives. Every year, her sales had been declining, and she was now at risk of being demoted or even let go. She was highly intelligent and very personable. When I asked her about her approach to client development, she said, "My clients know what I do and if they need me, they'll call me." That was my first clue that she had a self-limiting mindset that was the cause of her deteriorating performance.

Another client of mine started out each meeting with a new prospect by walking through a very slick, detailed PowerPoint presentation of his company's background and services. If the client interrupted or tried to shift the conversation away from his presentation, or asked too many questions, he got flustered. He would just obliviously power on with his slide deck. He believed that more product information and more displays of expertise would build more credibility and trust with his clients. But they didn't.

## The limitations of the "expert" mindset

Both of these individuals had what I call the "expert-for-hire" mindset. It is a narrow, me-centered, limiting mindset that will hold you back and even sabotage your success. It can lead you to overwhelm clients with breathless serenades about your products and services, your methodologies, and the details of your resume.

It also gives you tunnel vision. In 1980, for example, the old AT&T commissioned a top consulting firm to estimate the market for cell phones in the year 2000. Their answer: there would be 900,000 cell phones. They were only off by 108 million! The experts lacked the imagination to see the potential for mobile phones, and AT&T missed a huge opportunity to be an early entrant in this fast-growing business.

Harry Truman, who was president of the United States after Franklin D. Roosevelt, foreshadowed this when he quipped, "An expert is a fellow who's afraid to learn anything new, because then he wouldn't be an expert anymore." This gets at the notion that when we're experts, we want to stay within our narrow expertise at all times.

## The expansiveness of the "advisor" mindset

To see possibilities, you need the wide-angle lens of what I call the advisor mindset. With it, you provide clients with an expansive outlook on their problems and the potential solutions. Experts see themselves as specialists. Advisors also have deep expertise, but they layer breadth on top of their depth. They develop a robust knowledge of their client as an individual, of the client's business and organization, and the industry they operate in. They always frame their solutions in the context of the client's overall goals, strategies, and plans.

When you have the expert mindset you tend to talk *at* your client and focus on your extensive expertise. Your selling approach is to enthusiastically pitch *your* solutions With the advisor mindset, in contrast, you ask thought-provoking questions and listen deeply. You engage others in a discussion about *their* most critical issues. While experts strive to demonstrate professional credibility, advisors cultivate deep, personal trust. Experts are for hire, but advisors will push back and say "no" when it's appropriate to do so.

Experts usually accept the client's definition of their challenge. Where possible, however, advisors work with their clients to reframe it in order to define the total problem and the total solution. The result is greater impact and more value. All in all, when you have the expert mindset you tend to focus singularly on the transaction. Advisors takes a broader outlook, putting great value on the long-term relationship. Even when there are no fees coming in, they still add value to their client and behave like a trusted counselor.

The risk of not making this shift is grave. You'll be a tradable commodity who is one of many solid "experts" or product salespeople that clients can choose from. A plumber instead of a doctor. You'll think small, be reactive, and settle for a diet of small sales—of little mice.

A lioness, however, cannot live on mice alone—she simply can't catch enough of them each day to survive!

## When clients are just friends

I had a very savvy client who was a national managing partner for one of the Big 4 accounting firms. We were having dinner once, and he bemoaned the fact that some of the partners who worked for him had lots of relationships but never sold much. "They are always telling me about the great meetings they have with their client, and how terrific the relationship is," he confided. "But they never meet their revenue goals!"

He added, "I call that a '*friend*,' not a client!"

So my final point is this: You absolutely need a relationship orientation if you want to succeed with clients and build consultative relationships with senior executives. But you also need a *will to win*. This is reflected in a drive to do your utmost for each and every client. It's what pushes you to work late into the evening to make sure you are delivering the best possible quality or writing the most effective proposal. This will to win doesn't allow you to feel neutral about a competitor beating you out for a client contract. In fact, you hate it when that happens.

If you have a will to win, you are also motivated to study and train so that when you're in the crucible with your client, you're as prepared as you can possibly be.

My client summed it up at the end our dinner: "You need a certain hunger to succeed with clients. Some people don't have it—it's just not there. Without that hunger, even if you've got good skills, you're not going to truly shine."

## The essential combination

Figure 0.1 illustrates four combinations of these two essential attributes: a *relationship orientation* and a *will to win*.

If you're passive and simply react to individual client requests as they come along, you're an order taker.

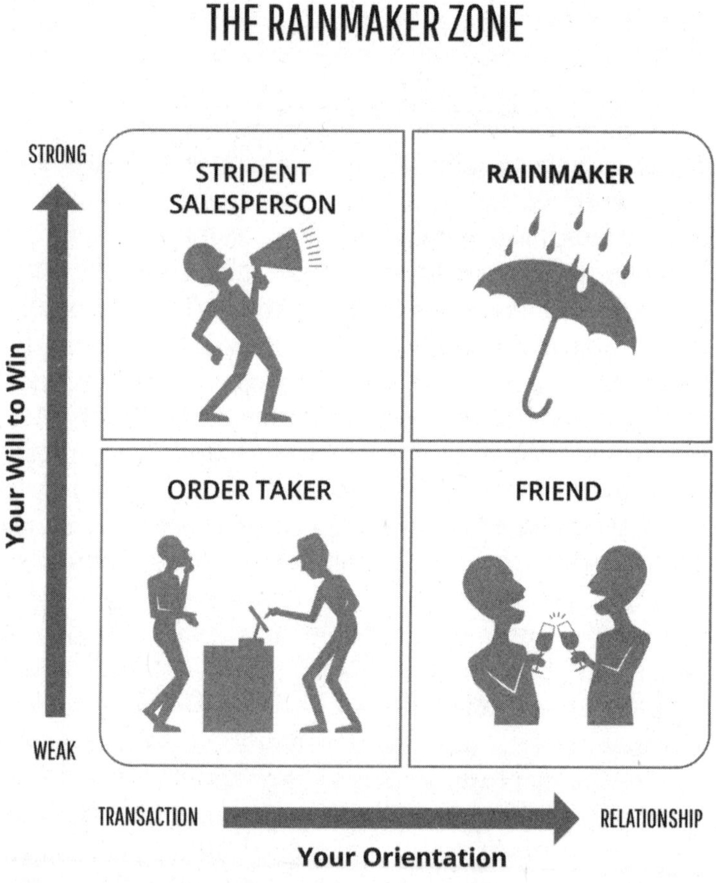


**Figure 0.1** The rainmaker zone

If you have a strong will to win, but lack a relationship focus, you're in the upper-left quadrant. You'll act like a strident, win-at-any-costs salesperson. You can do well here. But over time, you won't build the long-term trust and relational resilience that help anchor a great career.

Perhaps you have a relationship orientation but struggle to move the conversation along and identify a problem you can help your client solve. That can become more like friendship. You're in the lower-right quadrant, where the commercial relationship is weak or nonexistent.

If you powerfully combine a will to win with a strong relationship focus, that puts you in the upper-right quadrant. In that position, you assiduously develop deep, trusted relationships with your clients. You are driven to add great value to them. You frequently ponder what you can do to improve their business and how you can serve them better. When you find a critical issue to latch onto, you are tenacious. Here, you act as a true rainmaker.

The will to win, of course, must be equaled by the will to train to win. I know lots of people who want to succeed, make an impact, and become wealthy. But some of them are not willing to put in the time and effort to learn the skills that will get them those things.

If you love working with clients in the first place, you can develop and strengthen your hunger to succeed. Often, when we are empowered with the right skills and tools, it frees up our passion. After you read this book, I think you'll know where you stand.

**ADDITIONAL FREE RESOURCES FOR YOU**

Download my free *Client Growth Guide* at www.andrewsobel.com/growth-guide. It includes the self-assessment, Do You Have the Expert or Advisor Mindset, as well as dozens of other practical strategies and tools for growing your client base.

# Week 1 Choose Your Target

A client of mine, a large global bank, decided to conduct a review of their corporate banking relationships. This bank had been in business for over 100 years, and as you can imagine, had accumulated all manner of clients around the world. They discovered they had over 30,000 of them. Many were not profitable, however. Others were with companies that were a lousy fit with the bank's new strategy. Yet another group of these clients had developed marginally acceptable risk profiles. My client had become a hoarder of relationships. The result was a hornet's nest of problems.

Another client I worked with had a different but equally vexing problem with their client base. Over a three-year period, two large companies they served had dramatically increased their demand, and they now accounted for 60% of my client's revenue—a dangerous dependency. In addition, they turned out to be exceedingly difficult clients to work with. They demanded steep price discounts and treated my client poorly. Just as we set out on a strategy to broaden their revenue base, one of the two large clients came on hard times and cancelled half their orders.

My client survived, but it was a tough blow. The incident made them realize that *their* ideal client was a mid-sized company, not a large public corporation. When they refocused and also broadened their revenue base, their growth and profitability began to dramatically improve. And, their people were much, much happier.

As these examples illustrate, the composition of your client base is often the result of historical accident and short-term decision making rather than intentional strategic choice. Doing business with anyone who will write a check is an appealing strategy when you need to pay the bills or meet your sales target. But it's a formula for big trouble further down the road.

Good client relationships are like good meals—if you start with fresh, high-quality ingredients, you'll usually end up with a delicious dish. But try making a salad in January with those rock-hard winter tomatoes you buy in the supermarket—you know, the ones that are like golf balls. Ugh. It's not going to be great.

Pick your clients wisely from the start. Your chances of building long-term, rewarding relationships will vastly improve. The sale will go faster. Trust will quickly develop. You'll partner well together. Your client will get the results they seek. And you'll have a rewarding experience.

Let's walk through four simple steps that will help ensure you end up with the right clients.

## Know your value proposition

To know which clients make sense for you, you must understand the value you are offering the marketplace. So step one is to develop a clear *value proposition.* Can you succinctly articulate how you help clients? What outcomes do they achieve when they use your services or products? Sometimes we forget that what clients actually buy is a business *result* that is delivered by the solutions you sell.

Michelin tire company is a case in point. In 1947 they introduced the long-wearing radial tire. Michelin heavily promoted the technological superiority of radials, but the new tire never gained traction in the US market—it was a flop. Finally, in the 1970s they began focusing their advertising on the fact that you could drive many *more miles* on a set of radial tires. Radials quickly displaced standard bias tires and now account for virtually 100% of the market. Drivers didn't really care about the technology in the tires—they wanted more mileage on them, and they were willing to pay extra for it!

### Examples of value propositions

How would you articulate your or your company's value proposition? My principal one is this: *I help companies and individuals build their clients for life.*

Here are a few examples of value propositions (or in some cases, missions) from well-known organizations:

- "We help organizations across the private, public, and social sectors create the change that matters." (McKinsey & Company)
- "Remember everything." (Evernote)
- "To organize the world's information and make it universally accessible and useful." (Google)
- "We empower every person and every organization on the planet to achieve more." (Microsoft)

- "We ignite opportunity by setting the world in motion." (Uber)
- "Accenture solves our clients' toughest challenges by providing unmatched services in strategy, consulting, digital, technology and operations." (Accenture)

Some of the these are fairly broad, because these companies do many things for their clients and customers. The more focused your service offering, the more specific your value proposition can be. My friend Marshall Goldsmith, the executive coach and bestselling author, says, "I help successful people achieve positive, lasting change in behavior; for themselves, their people, and their teams."

Next, you have to identify your target clients. You should use three sequential screens or filters to assess whether or not a client makes sense for you.

## Screen for strategic fit

Strategic fit refers to a set of criteria you have established to define your target market—that is, the clients who really need what you offer. These criteria could specify:

- Types of industries
- Company size
- Private, public, or governmental organizations
- Geographic location
- Wholesale (B2B) or retail (B2C) businesses
- Companies with certain well-developed functions that you specialize in (e.g., operations, IT, logistics, etc.)
- Other characteristics that would make these clients heavy users of your solutions and value (e.g., capital intensive vs. labor intensive, domestic vs. international, companies that spend a lot on training versus those that don't, how often they relocate their staff, etc.)

If you aren't clear on which prospective clients fit your strategy, you'll tend to take on any client who will pay your bill. The result will be a mélange that will eventually dilute your performance and impact.

One of my clients decided to use their reward system to encourage adherence to their target client definition. They made a list of 1,000 companies, and their people only got credit for sales to those organizations. That sounds harsh, but it dramatically focused their efforts and improved their profitability.

Large multinationals with comprehensive offerings can, of course, go after a broad range of clients. But if you're a smaller firm or solo practitioner, you need to think through your screening criteria pretty carefully. Otherwise you'll end up like my bank client, a hoarder of relationships.

The deeper your knowledge of a particular industry, market, process, or type of company, the more differentiated your expertise will be and the stronger your ability to compete. As an example, I have spent decades deepening my knowledge of an important process—how to develop and grow client relationships—and so I screen for clients who are trying to build trusted, consultative relationships with senior executives. Someone else's focus would likely be completely different and, I hope, uniquely matched to their particular strategy.

---

What types of clients represent the best strategic fit with you and your firm, given the type of value you add and the solutions you provide?

---

## Screen for relational fit

Because I believe strongly in the importance of relationships—in business and in life—I want to know whether I can have a positive, trusted relationship with a prospective client. I also want assurance that the client's reputation will enhance—or at least not diminish—my own! Here are some questions you should ask to test for relational fit:

- *Does the client have a history of building productive, long-term relationships with external providers?* Wouldn't you prefer a client who has a healthy relationship orientation, versus one who treats everyone like an arms-length, disposable vendor?
- *Does this organization have a good reputation?* Your own image is strongly affected by your clients' standing in the marketplace. If you find a client taking ethical or legal shortcuts, head for the door.
- *Are the leadership and the company culture aligned with or at least not in conflict with your core values?* Every three or four years I encounter a client whose values and general outlook are so at odds with my own that I have to diplomatically wind things down or let the engagement peter out.
- *Do you sense, from the very first meeting, that you will be treated with courtesy and respect?* Some clients are tough during the sales process, but then love you to death once they accept your proposal. But usually, what you experience on Day 1 is what you will probably get six months later.

## Screen for your ability to have an impact

If a client fits both your strategic and relational selection criteria, you then have to ask, "Will I be able to have an impact?" Sometimes, the circumstances are such that can't really add value, and you end up banging your head against a wall.

If you don't have a visible impact, you probably won't have an enthusiastic client who is referring you to others. So screen for this right from the start.

Do you know one of the secrets behind surgeons who have high success rates with their patients? They are careful to only accept patients who are excellent candidates for their particular procedure.

**WHEN TO BE FLEXIBLE ABOUT CLIENT SELECTION**

Are you at the beginning of your career or just starting a new business? You may have to be more flexible about how you apply your three client filters. Sometimes, you really do just need to pay the bills. Or you may simply need a few reference-able clients to get off the ground and spread word-of-mouth. If you work for a large firm, you may not have much choice about which clients you work with—that will often be decided for you, based on your firm's client targeting strategy.

Later in your career, however, you should be increasingly selective about your clients. You only have so many working hours in a week, and your professional life is finite. Where are you going to have the biggest impact? How will you leave a legacy?

Here are four principal factors you should assess to determine the potential for impact.

1. First, is it the *right issue*? Is the problem causing serious pain? Is the client determined to address it? Is the issue in your sweet spot as a firm?
2. Second, are you dealing with the *right executives*? Do they have the organization's respect and the authority to support and sponsor you and your company? Can they make a decision to buy? Are they able to gain support from other parts of the organization, which may be affected by your product or service?
3. Third, is the client *large enough*—or might it reasonably be in the future—to support your ambitions? Small clients can be valuable in a number of ways, but they can also deplete your time and energy while yielding little return.

4. Fourth, does the client have *strong leadership*? An ambitious, well-managed client is usually a pleasure to work with. It should be able to successfully implement your solutions. A client that is disorganized, politicized, and lacks coherent leadership at the top, however, can be a nightmare.

How many of your current clients would pass these three screens—strategic fit, relational fit, and impact?

Figure 1.1 summarizes the client screening process.

## The magic word

One of your biggest problems in selecting the right clients may be the inability to say "no." There will always be pressures to say "yes," even when it's not in your long-term interests to do so.

There will be pressure from the client to lower your prices and accept their offer "just this once" or "to help build a relationship with us." Pressure from your manager or boss to say yes to whatever the client wants. Pressure to meet your revenue goals. Pressure to help finish the year on a strong note. Pressure from your psyche to say *yes* so you can feel good about getting a sale, or so you'll feel liked and wanted. Believe me, I've experienced all these emotions, and more.

Billionaire Warren Buffet is the CEO of Berkshire Hathaway and one of the world's wealthiest investors. He hangs out with a lot of successful people—Microsoft cofounder Bill Gates is one of his best friends. Buffet said this about the power of "no":

> "The difference between successful people and really successful people is that really successful people say no to almost everything."

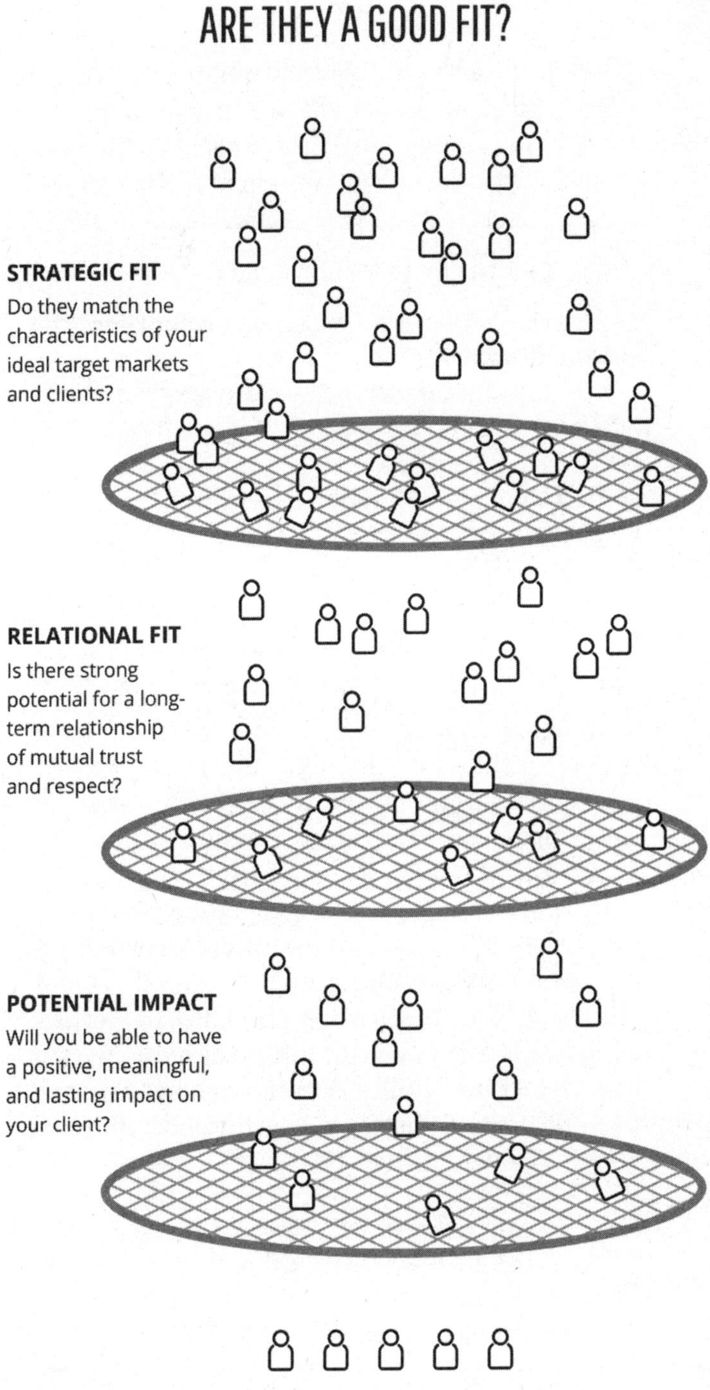


**Figure 1.1** Are they a good fit?

This doesn't mean you should say no to almost all your clients! But you get the point. The way you end up with a portfolio of great clients is to be very discerning about which clients you bring on board to begin with.

**PUTTING KEY IDEAS INTO ACTION**

- Create clarity about the value you offer clients by writing down your value proposition. What benefit or value do clients derive from your solutions *and* from having a relationship with you?
- Test out and refine your value proposition with some of your best clients. Does it resonate with them? Does it correspond to their own view of what you offer?
- *Strategic fit:* Write down the criteria for your ideal client in terms of size, industry, location, type of operations, and so on. Then, assess how many of your current clients match those criteria. What does this tell you?
- *Relational fit:* What are the characteristics of your ideal client from a relational perspective? I listed some earlier that might also be meaningful for you, such as a history of positive relationships and respect for your expertise. Create your own list. Again, what percentage of your current clients would pass your screen?
- *Potential for impact:* For you, what are the ideal conditions that allow you to have a positive, lasting impact on your clients? What percentage of your current clients meet these conditions? Could you change or renegotiate elements of those relationships that don't stack up to your criteria (e.g., increase the scope, connect at more senior levels) and increase your impact?
- Review your prospects and clients. Is there anyone—or any project—you should be saying "no" to?

# Week 2 Get Recognized

In the 2006 Oscar-winning movie *Little Miss Sunshine*, Greg Kinnear plays Richard, an aspiring motivational speaker and author. It's a wonderful, funny movie that also stars comedian Steve Carell. In a side plot, Richard has developed a program for personal success based on nine steps. He's run out of money, however, to support his family. His financial salvation rests on publishing a book about his success formula.

Stan Grossman, Richard's literary agent, has promised to get Richard a large advance on the book. But suddenly, he stops returning his calls. Desperate, Richard crashes a publishing conference Stan is attending and confronts him next to the swimming pool. When Richard realizes he has no book deal, he angrily shouts, "But it's a great program!" And Stan replies, "It's not the program. It's *you. No one has heard of you.* Nobody cares." Richard's dreams are crushed.

It's just a movie, but that scene is very real. You need to be recognized for something in order to attract relationships and business, whether it's to get a book deal or win new clients. Sure, if you represent a well-known company, it's much easier to get in the door—*the first time.* But your firm's brand alone, although valuable, is not sufficient to make you truly successful. It can get you the first meeting, and it will secure invitations to competitive bids. But it's your own brand—your recognition—that attracts the inbound interest from clients that leads to follow-on sales and sole-source business.

## You need recognition and renown to attract clients

I've interviewed thousands of executives on their use of external suppliers and advisors. Here are some very typical comments they've made to me about who they are willing to meet with:

- "If you get into my office, it's because you've already been screened."
- "Generally speaking, I will not meet with an external provider I don't already know, unless they have been specifically recommended to me by a colleague or friend."
- "I make time for people and firms who I know have a track record of success."
- "We are able to be very choosy about who we work with, and we pick the best in their fields."
- "You need to show that you have something to offer—an idea, a solution—that will help me achieve my key priorities. Of course, I'm a lot more open to meeting if I already know you or know of you, or if you've been recommended to me by someone I trust."

Don't rely solely on your firm's brand. *You* have to develop recognition as well.

Simply put, if you have no visibility in your chosen market—no reputation for expertise—it's hard to get in front of buyers and build a client base. At best you'll be fighting it out in grueling competitive bids, where you'll be one of five companies submitting proposals. And at worst, you'll struggle to gin up enough business to survive.

## Access is harder than ever

In many ways, gaining access, especially to senior executives, is tougher than ever. Top executives are time-starved. Many could fill 24 hours each day with appointments with all the people who want to see them. Consequently, they stringently guard their calendars.

One of my first consulting assignments involved interviewing the heads of IT at major retail store chains. There was no Internet, so I had to research their names and telephone numbers in printed directories (yes, I survived doing business without a smartphone and laptop . . . and even enjoyed more time to think and reflect). The vast majority were happy to speak with me and do an interview. Today, that direct approach would fail. To reach such executives, you would need to be introduced by someone they trusted and/or be a recognized expert in your field.

The counterweight to the inaccessibility of executives is the ability the Internet gives us to connect with people. We can now approach clients in many different ways, such as through LinkedIn, by commenting on a blog or article they wrote, texting them, or even just with plain old email.

However, regardless of the technology you use to get in touch, there are two important, enabling factors: recognition and value. Executives are likely to agree to speak with me if they know who I am and/or if they perceive they'll get some value out of the conversation. Recognition is correlated with *expected value.* So, no matter how clever you are at using technology tools to track people down, you won't get anywhere if you don't have something of value to offer the other person.

## Climbing the recognition ladder

Summarizing the arc of celebrity fame, the actor Hugh O'Brien wrote this in a letter to a Hollywood gossip columnist in 1960:

1. Who is Hugh O'Brien?
2. Get me Hugh O'Brien.
3. Get me someone who is a Hugh O'Brien type.
4. Get me a young Hugh O'Brien.
5. Who WAS Hugh O'Brien?

There is a definite lifecycle to your notoriety, which I can personally attest to. I hope, however, I haven't reached the final stage of Hugh O'Brien's typology!

But all humor aside, there are three principal levels of recognition that you can and should strive for.

### Level one: Internal recognition

After a year at my first consulting firm, my then-girlfriend and I decided to get married (so far so good—this is our 37th year together). At the time, however, I was living and working in Boston, and she was employed in the international division of a bank in New York City. So we hatched a plan to end up in the same city.

I heard our CEO and founder, James Kelly, was planning to move to London to start an office there. I approached James and made a pitch to help him start the office. I brought some modest qualifications: I spoke three foreign languages reasonably well and had prior experience living abroad. Perhaps more importantly, in the space of a year, I had made friends in the firm. I performed well on my projects, worked hard, and pitched in when anyone needed help.

After checking carefully with other partners, James called me up and said he'd be delighted to have me move to London as part of the startup team. At the same time, my fiancé asked her bank if they would also transfer her to London (instead of Paris, which was where they had planned to send her). They said "yes" to her as well.

Getting both our employers to move us to London, at the same time, felt like a supernatural event. But the explanation is much simpler: We had both achieved internal recognition, and this opened up a great opportunity for us.

Internal recognition creates new career breaks for you and, in particular, opportunities to earn client recognition. In any company, leadership will often put people with the best reputations for delivering results into high-profile, client-facing roles.

Fundamentally, internal recognition grows when you build key relationships and add value to the organization. This means:

- Consistently delivering quality work and achieving your goals.
- Developing an in-demand expertise.
- Being seen as a team player—someone who collaborates well and willingly helps out colleagues when they need a hand (but not a doormat).
- Building trusted relationships with key stakeholders such as your manager, colleagues, senior executives, mentors, and so on.

What are the signs of strong internal recognition? For example: you get regular promotions and pay increases, you have the clout to influence your work assignments, you are asked to join committees and task forces, and more senior executives seek you out for their teams.

### Level two: Client recognition

What's the difference between just doing client work and getting *client recognition*?

Here are some important signs that indicate you've gone beyond just being an expert resource that clients use on a transactional basis:

- You routinely win repeat business from your clients.
- When your clients are surveyed or interviewed by your management, they specifically cite your good work and ask for you to continue working on their account.
- When a client executive moves to another company, they call you up and want to continue doing business with you and your firm.
- Clients tell others about you and refer their friends and colleagues to you.

A senior manager I know at a major firm, Josh, is considered a top performer. His boss tells me he's on the fast track to become a partner. His secret? *Visible client recognition.*

Josh, who is in his mid-30s, gets glowing reports when his firm's leadership interview his clients, who specifically request him for new projects. He also gets calls from past clients who want to do more business with him and his firm. Other executives, who have heard about his work through word-of-mouth, also periodically get in touch.

"When I first started working with clients," he told me, "I had a kind of 'humble servant' attitude. But then I realized most clients actually want a trusted partner who is dedicated to them but *also* willing to push back and give them the unvarnished truth. So I changed my style, and it transformed my relationships. Now, I approach clients as peers and they use me as a sounding board. I have also found that being caring is essential—you have to show you care about them as people and you want them to succeed. Part of that is just being human—I can say, in response to a client's question, 'I don't know. But I'll get you an answer tomorrow.' That honesty makes you more authentic."

He added: "When the client's formulation of the problem is too narrow, I push back. Sometimes, I say, 'To get the result you need, we need to step back and look at a broader scope.' This gives me a lot of credibility—I'm not just taking orders."

There are six distinct focal points you can utilize to strengthen your client recognition:

1. *Industry.* By specializing in an industry, you build deep experience in how your solutions are uniquely used by clients in that industry.
2. *Function or Process.* If your solutions help improve a function (like HR or finance) or a process (like financial transaction processing or sales), you can go very deep into it and build your network with like-minded executives who work in those areas.
3. *Intellectual Capital.* When you have an intellectual capital focus, you create interesting ideas and solutions to client challenges. You then get them out into the marketplace through articles, online posts, books, speeches, and so forth. If your content is good, clients will seek you out. A prime example is the consulting firm McKinsey. Early in its history, the firm developed the *McKinsey Quarterly*, a scholarly journal distributed to top executives around the world. "Knowledge creation" is in fact a key value and performance indicator in the firm.

4. *Large Clients.* An entire career can be built around just a handful of large clients. You must be highly relationship-focused, get to know a client's organization extremely well, and build a network with multiple buyers.
5. *In-Person Social Networking.* Some professionals—often extroverts—excel at social networking. They are always "in the flow," hosting dinners, joining associations and clubs, going to cultural events, attending various happenings, and getting involved in nonprofit causes. They use these connections to meet decision-makers in prospective client organizations. Introverts can thrive at this sort of networking, too, but may do better one-on-one or in small groups.
6. *Geography.* Whether you live in Houston, Atlanta, Rome, or Budapest, there are many opportunities to develop roots into the local community and focus on potential clients in your city. Of course, you'll bring some functional or industry expertise, but a distinct geographic focus can be a valuable complement to the other five models.

You may very well use several of these focal points. For example, I focus on intellectual capital development (#3) and the process of relationship building (#2), and also have acquired deep experience in several industries (#1).

Remember: the more specific your focus, the easier it is to develop recognition and renown.

### Level three: External recognition (the media and other thought leaders)

Three or four times a month I get unsolicited requests from diverse media outlets to do interviews or contribute to an article. Someone is usually writing about a topic that intersects with my known area of expertise, and through either Internet searches or speaking with colleagues, they come up with my name. This doesn't happen by accident. Over the last 20 years I've published a large number of books and articles, spoken at conferences around the world, and contributed content to hundreds of websites and many different publications.

Your reaction may be, "That's just not me. I don't write and publish the way you do."

But let me push you on this point. There are many benefits from media recognition of your expertise and success. The cumulative impact of reaching level three produces, to use a term popularized by author Alan Weiss, "marketing gravity." When you have marketing gravity, rather than being forced to cold-call clients to drum up business, clients are drawn toward you by the gravitational pull of your renown.

Furthermore, we live in a low-trust world where suppliers make many inflated claims about their products and services. Media recognition builds clients' trust in you by providing what are effectively powerful, third-party endorsements of you and your work. The late critics Roger Ebert and Gene Siskel, for example, did this through

**WHERE DO YOU NEED TO BE ON THE RECOGNITION LADDER?**

Early on in your career, your focus should largely be on levels one and two—internal and client recognition. You need to make sure you are deepening your expertise and strengthening your most important relationships during this period.

As your career advances, it's critical to ascend to level three, where you attract recognition from other thought leaders and by the media.

In practice, you don't move in a straight line, linearly, through the three levels of recognition. You might even work on all three levels at once, simultaneously building your internal recognition, your reputation for quality work with clients, and also your media recognition.

their "thumbs up" or "thumbs down" movie ratings. Same with the J.D. Power automotive quality rankings. If you are on a panel at a well-known business conference, the halo of prestige from that event also lights you up.

How do you know you've reached level three recognition? When a journalist or writer is researching a story in your area of expertise, you come up on their radar. Other experts might ask to interview you for their own publications, blogs, and podcasts. If a prospective client searches for you on the Internet, publications you've authored come up. Perhaps you receive recognition or awards from within your profession—for example, a client of mine was recently asked to join his profession's national accreditation board.

## If you can't write it, can you really think it?

There are additional reasons why you should *aspire* to Level Three recognition. These have to do with the writing and speaking that are such an important part of getting recognized.

First, writing and speaking are powerful disciplines that sharpen your thinking and crystalize your insights. Write a short article, blog, or white paper on a topic. Put time into it and produce something of quality. You'll find you are then *vastly* more incisive and persuasive. You'll crackle with energy and clarity when you talk to a client about that subject. Writing and speaking raise your game.

Second, our minds are always searching for evidence that lines up with our existing beliefs. When you share insights with your clients through formal writing and speaking, it amplifies the esteem they have for you. It reinforces their existing positive feelings about your value to them.

Third, when you write and speak, it stimulates your creativity and positive thinking. In 2005, the National Science Foundation published an article that states that the average person has around 12,000 to 60,000 thoughts each day. Eighty percent of them are negative and 95% are repetitive—they are the same thoughts as the day before. That's a discouraging, but not surprising, finding. By taking the time to develop and sharpen your points of view, however, you can get out of this rut and freshen your ideas.

Additionally, there's research that shows we *do not* learn much from experience. It's sad but true: We often do the same tasks every day at work, without much learning or creative thought. Writing and speaking are two powerful ways to counter this.

Finally, writing down your insights forces you to engage in what author Cal Newport calls "Deep Work." It's when you isolate yourself from distractions and focus all your attention on exploring a specific professional issue or problem. Deep Work is increasingly uncommon in a world that is designed to constantly distract you and where multi-tasking—which is a terribly inefficient way to use your brain—is a badge of honor.

## Typical challenges you may encounter

You're bound to hit some obstacles on the road to building your recognition. I spoke to author Dorie Clark about some of the most common challenges people face. Clark has written several acclaimed books on building your personal brand, including *Stand Out* and *Entrepreneurial You.*

"One barrier I often hear about from younger professionals," she says, "is the manager or boss who isn't keen for you to be building your network and gaining personal recognition. In this situation, a good strategy is to develop relationships horizontally, across your organization. Get yourself on a cross-functional team or committee, which is far less threatening to your boss than going over their head and schmoozing with top management." For a young financial consultant I interviewed for this book, this was exactly her strategy. She became part of a practice development committee in the New York office of her firm and made invaluable connections with other colleagues—and also some partners—who were involved in the effort.

Another challenge is feeling like you don't have enough to say or are not sufficiently expert in something. Clark's rejoinder is this: "People often feel like they need a mythical level of expertise to write or speak about a topic. It's not true. You need to reframe it as simply sharing your ideas and being helpful to others." If you're very early in your career, Clark points out that a good strategy is to interview someone who is an experienced, deep expert, and write about what you learn from him or her.

Think about this not as "coming up with an amazing idea" but rather "making your implicit knowledge explicit." I remember a young participant in one of my workshops who worked with companies in the educational sector. He said he had nothing to write about. I asked him, "I'm curious, do you think Millennials (born 1981–1996) like to learn in different ways than Baby Boomers (born 1946–1964)? He immediately began rattling off some very interesting points about how younger professionals absorb new knowledge. I challenged him to turn what he had just said into a one-pager. He later sent it to me—"Five Ways Millennials Like to Learn"—and told me that short piece had fueled half a dozen very vibrant meetings with clients and prospects.

What implicit knowledge and experience can you make explicit for your clients?

## It's not just about meeting the right people

There's a lot of hype these days about how the key to success is networking to meet the right kinds of people. The media glorifies this idea. Usually the turning point in someone's rags-to-riches story is a chance meeting with a pivotal figure who opens a door and changes her life forever.

But don't forget two important truths. First, the best way to attract "the right people" into a relationship with you is to have something of value to offer them and build a reputation as someone who helps others succeed. Second, there are between 15 and 25 people who will have a huge, disproportionate impact on your career success. You need to identify them and intentionally deepen your relationships with them.

The "amazing, providential meeting" storyline makes for good print. Most people's success, however, is due to something more prosaic. It's the culmination of much hard work to hone their craft. It's based on their concerted efforts to develop trusted relationships with their clients, managers, colleagues, thought leaders in their field, and other key stakeholders.

You should absolutely network and meet new people. Never forget, however, the importance of your "critical few." These are the trusted relationships with 15 to 25 key individuals who will really make a difference in your career.

**PUTTING KEY IDEAS INTO ACTION**

- Develop internal recognition by building a reputation for helping others succeed. Remember Dale Carnegie's famous quote: "You can make more friends in two months by becoming interested in other people than you can in two years trying to get others interested in you." Start by learning the priorities and goals of the people in your professional life.
- Rate your client recognition using a scale of 1 to 5, where 1 = Almost no recognition, and 5 = Very high recognition. What would your score be for current clients? For the overall client market you serve?
- Write down one or two key areas of expertise that you want to be known for. What are three or four steps you can take, in the next six to nine months, to deepen your knowledge of these topics? Put these activities into your calendar. Also write down three or four personal qualities that you want to be part of your own personal brand. Complete this sentence: "If asked, my clients would say my most outstanding qualities are X, Y, and Z. . . ."
- Make your implicit knowledge explicit. Pick a common problem or challenge your clients face, write it down, and then list four or five strategies to address it. This can be just 400 to 500 words—like a blog entry. One simple, short piece alone can create five or 10 interesting client conversations for you.
- Write a minimum of one short article or white paper every month. In a year you'll have 12 interesting thought-starters that you can share with clients, publish online, post on LinkedIn, or submit to publications in a longer article format.

Figure 2.1 illustrates the dozens of ways you can gain recognition.

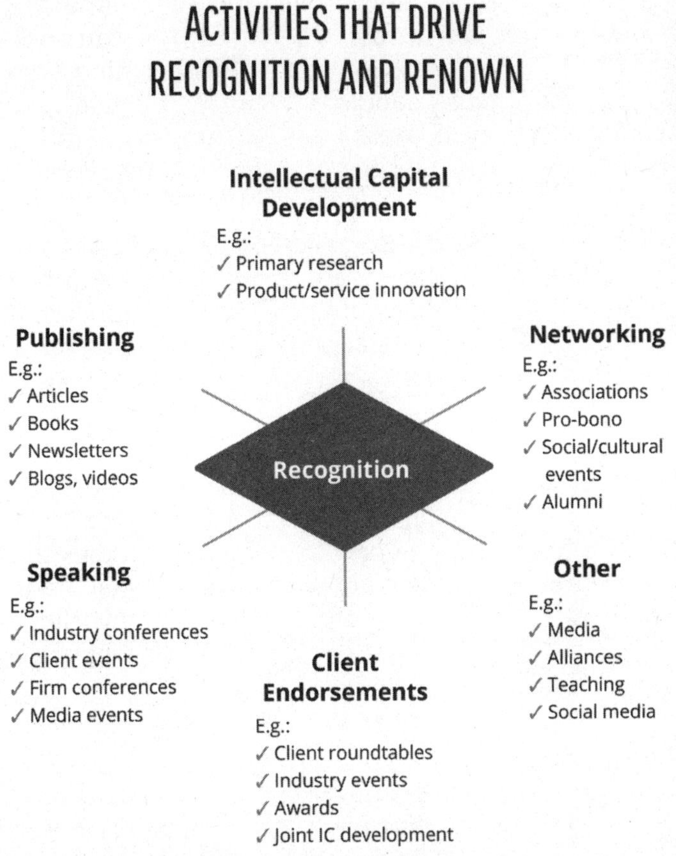


**Figure 2.1** Activities that drive recognition and renown

# Week 3 Find Your Clients

When my old firm appointed me as the country CEO for Italy, the business there had shrunk to just $500,000 dollars in revenue and a couple of consultants. It was underwater.

My mandate was to grow the practice and integrate it with the rest of our company. The situation was dire, however. If I didn't quickly build up the client base and get some revenues, we would drown under the weight of fixed costs for offices and staff.

Within two years we had grown the business to $6 million, and after four years it reached $12 million and 45 staff—over $20 million in today's dollars. As a comeback challenge, it went well.

While there were many dimensions to the turnaround, it boiled down to five strategies that my team and I intentionally pursued.

## Use multiple channels to reach clients

There was no "one way" that we used to find new clients. I started by assessing the current but rather limited list of clients. First, we held client account planning sessions to look at opportunities to sell additional services and expand these relationships—those were our best, short-term opportunities for new revenue. Second, I built or strengthened relationships with what I call collaborators, who could introduce us to new clients—in this case, well-known business school professors and other university faculty the firm had a connection to in Italy. Third, I looked at opportunities to meet with the Italian operations of multinational clients that the firm was doing business with in other parts of the world. And fourth, I sat down with my Italian partner, who was well-connected in Italy, and made a list of executives we could go talk to. Between all of these sources, we quickly built a sales funnel of promising leads.

Notice that I did not tell you that I cold-called people I didn't know. I always, somehow, got warm introductions. I would search and ask and invariably find someone who knew someone who could help me get the meeting I wanted.

## Build your network before you need it

I took a long-term view of each potential relationship. Sure, in my discussions with executives I was always driving to identify a possible client challenge that we could address. But in many cases I simply got to know people, learned about their issues, and tried to be helpful! One executive I called on was the then-CEO of the burgeoning wireless phone company in Italy. I met with him repeatedly over a one-year period, sharing ideas about how to improve his business. Nothing ever developed in that year. But I kept at it.

During one conversation, he seemed very agitated, and I asked him if he had something on his mind. He told me his 18-year-old daughter was going to spend the summer in London, and he was extremely worried. She had no job and no plans. So I offered to introduce her to the manager of our London office, Jackie, to see whether she could give his daughter any advice or leads. It turned out we were moving offices that summer, and Jackie needed some extra hands to help with the move. So she provided a kind of internship for the daughter.

The next month I got a call from the CEO. He said, "Mr. Sobel, I think there's something you can help me with." That small, initial project led to a $1 million annual relationship. I didn't offer to help his daughter with the expectation of currying his favor or getting a project—I honestly did it to be helpful. I care about other people, and it was a natural response to the CEO's dilemma. For him, it cemented his professional and *personal* trust in me.

So build your network before you need it. Help others and develop a trusted relationship with them *before* you want something. And show you care. A caring, empathetic attitude will powerfully nurture your relationships.

### Develop flagship clients

In the first year, I was able to win what became two, multi-million-dollar clients. They provided the steady revenue that enabled us to hire new people and invest in marketing to win yet more new clients. They provided the "escape velocity" we needed to dramatically grow the business.

In the early days of its international expansion, the premier management consulting firm Bain & Company used the flagship strategy to build out its global network of offices rapidly, while maintaining high levels of profitability. In each city, they would aim to grow one major client—they referred to it as a "consolidated relationship." Then, and only then, would they actually set up an office with local hires.

One or two major client accounts will supercharge your business. Flagship clients provide a variety of benefits, including financial ballast, opportunities for intellectual capital innovation, reputational enhancement, and referrals to other great clients.

### Lead with value

There was another common theme to all of our client development efforts: *added value.* I feverishly packaged and repackaged my and my firm's thought leadership on topics of interest to the Italian companies I was calling on. I wrote articles, had them translated into Italian, and then pitched them to local publications and media. I shared best practices from our work with other companies in the same industries. And I always made sure I brought a couple of ideas to each client meeting. In the next chapter, I'll share more about the specific techniques that I use in first meetings to add value and build my credibility.

### Hire great people

Once I had secured some major new clients, we began to hire rapidly. We were able to pick up some great individuals, and they further reinforced our capabilities and growth. But . . . *it started with the clients.* Without those early client wins, we would not have had the resources to bring new people on board.

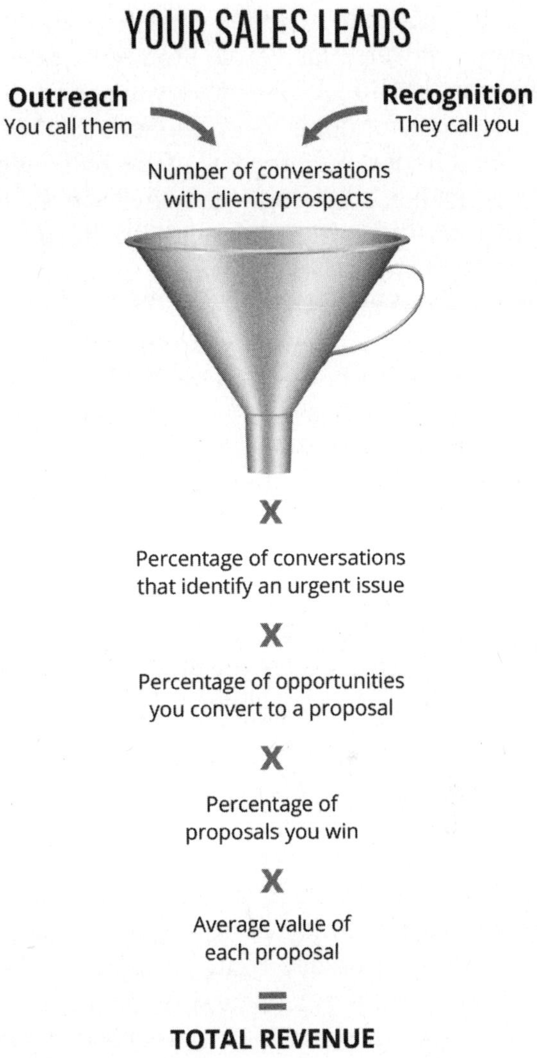


**Figure 3.1** Your sales leads

## Turn conversations into relationships and revenue

The importance of proactive outreach and recognition are illustrated in Figure 3.1. Have a careful look at it.

As you can see, there are five key stages in the journey from first conversation to sold proposal. At each stage, there are opportunities to improve your effectiveness—and I'll share tips for doing so throughout this book.

The *most* important thing I want you to focus on right now is the first box at the top—on increasing the number of conversations you are having with qualified prospects and clients. By *qualified* I mean one of three types of people: First, someone who is a buyer—a decision-maker who can authorize purchasing what you sell. Second, someone who can lead you to a buyer. And third, someone who can help prepare you for your meeting with the buyer.

Some of these you will procure through proactive outreach (you ask for a meeting). Some, I hope, will come directly to you, unsolicited, through the recognition you are building in the marketplace.

When you increase the number and quality of these first conversations, it dramatically strengthens the entire sales funnel and grows your revenue. They are the primary fuel for your client development.

## The hierarchy of client calls

One of my favorite *New Yorker* cartoons was drawn in 1993 by Robert Mankoff. It shows an executive at his desk, fielding a telephone call from someone who wants to meet him. "No, Thursday's out," he replies to the caller, adding, "How about never? Is never good for you?"

That wry, cynical phrase—"Is never good for you?" has now entered our popular language, and you'll see it quoted by politicians and celebrities alike. It feels all too real if you're trying to get meetings with busy top executives.

When you are trying to grow your business, where do you start? The old paradigm was to look where there was light—where the obvious names were. The problem is that you'll join a long queue of competitors at the door of these companies.

The best leads often arrive once you have established some recognition and renown among your existing clients and other prospects in the market you serve. This will lead to some inquiries that just come over the transom. It's powerful when executives call *you* to ask whether you can solve a problem or help capture an opportunity for them. You are already 50% of the way through the sales process when you get this type of inbound inquiry.

Below, I've listed 12 ways to get access. Read through these, and see which ones make the most sense for the executives you would like meet with.

## Platinum: Inspire inbound leads

1. **Existing client calls you.** You enable this through consistent, high-quality delivery. You also need to engage your client in regular agenda-setting discussions where you explore their emerging plans and priorities. Additionally, ensure your clients have an up-to-date understanding of your capabilities and solutions.
2. **Prospective client calls you.** This happens when you have built recognition in the marketplace for your expertise and thought leadership, encouraged your clients and other collaborators to share positive word-of-mouth about you, and built a reputation for working with leading companies and institutions.

## Gold: Create leads through outreach

3. **Proactively call a current client.** You should regularly meet with your current clients in order to step back from the day-to-day work and explore their agenda of key priorities, needs, and goals. Think of it as getting off the dance floor and taking a "balcony view" of their business. Your best prospects for near-term, new business are almost always your existing clients.

4. **Get referrals and other warm introductions to prospects.** Always strive to get a warm introduction to meet a prospective client. Most senior executives will only meet with a new provider if a colleague or friend has recommended them. Professional networking platforms like LinkedIn can be very helpful in figuring out who knows whom. Some companies are also using new software that identifies connections across the entire organization. Best of all, however, is an enthusiastic referral from a current client.
5. **Start with an online relationship.** An online relationship can be an effective prelude to a face-to-face meeting. You can comment on someone's blog or LinkedIn post, for example, and set up a dialogue. You can post a review of a book or article someone's written. Or just email them. Email is not dead. I get lots of it from people who have read one of my publications and want to strike up a conversation (my email address happens to be public—it's on my website, andrewsobel.com).

### HOW TO ENSURE PROSPECTS AND CLIENTS WILL *ALWAYS* TAKE A MEETING OR CALL WITH YOU

During a particularly tough year, a partner I knew at a large executive search firm told me he was having a hard time getting meetings. "Even old clients of mine don't want to see me," he said, adding, "They tell me, 'Don't bother, we're just not hiring right now!'"

The problem was that my friend's clients viewed him as a transactional expert, not someone who would be valuable to meet with *regardless* of whether they needed help finding a new hire. He simply wasn't adding enough value between search assignments.

You need to be at what I call "the crossroads of the marketplace." This means you're out meeting with lots of different interesting people, and are known for having engaging ideas and information to share. As a result, people will always be happy to meet with you.

The specific platforms for beginning an online relationship will, of course, evolve and further develop from whatever is in common use today (anyone remember MySpace or AOL Messenger?).

6. **Ask your leadership or CEO to set up a meeting.** If you work with a firm, you can sometimes get a meeting in the C-suite if one of your top leaders contacts the prospect or client.
7. **Start with a non-commercial relationship.** Some of my best relationships with senior executives have started this way. You might connect with an executive through a non-profit organization, by involving them in a research project, by interviewing them for an article or book, and so on. This is another reason to do research, write, and publish: It gives you an excuse to engage with senior executives and other thought leaders.
8. **Connect at a conference or professional event.** When I was earning my BA degree at Middlebury college, I used to fish quite often in the surrounding lakes and streams in Vermont and upstate New York. The big challenge, as any fisherman knows, was always: Where are the fish today? Are they deep? Near the surface? In a calm pool behind a large boulder? Similarly, you need to figure out where your particular buyers hang out. What conferences or events do they attend? What publications do they read? Scrutinize events carefully, however. One client of mine, a lawyer, stopped going to a big annual legal conference. He told me, "The only people who attend are other lawyers looking for business. It doesn't draw actual clients anymore!"
9. **Create a tailored event for that person.** When I suggested to a client of mine that they create a custom dinner event for a CEO they wanted to meet, they responded that she would never agree to attend. I said, "Remove all constraints. What would interest her in attending?" They admitted that they had heard the CEO was a huge fan of a particular author, a well-known historian. I

asked: "What would it be worth to your company to build a relationship with this CEO?" They admitted it would be a priceless connection to have. They got the point and hired the author to speak at a small, intimate dinner with just five clients. And the CEO agreed to come! You may not need to hire an expensive speaker—but do come up with ideas that align with the particular interests and goals of the person you want to meet.

10. **Write or call with a unique idea.** Many top executives have told me that they are quite discerning about making room in their schedules to hear a pitch from someone they don't know. The first exception is when that person is recommended to them. Another exception they cite is if that person appears to have an intriguing, new idea. "I'm always open to hearing an interesting idea," one CEO told me. "In fact," he continued, "earlier this year I got an email from a guy at a firm I didn't know very well. He had, however, an idea for our business that I found quite promising. So I agreed to meet." Another executive cautioned me: "The idea or solution has to squarely align with one of my key strategies or goals. I'm not interested in hearing about fascinating new products that aren't relevant to what I'm trying to accomplish."
11. **Bring them some potential business.** A great way to start a relationship is to bring a customer or business proposition to your prospect or client. One of my own clients, for example, came up with a business idea that involved forming a joint venture with a large multinational. The idea was successful. They created a new stream of revenue from the joint venture, *and* their partner in the new business became a major client for their services.
12. **Do something original and dramatic.** Years ago, one of my clients wanted to win Southwest Airlines as a client. They struggled, however, to get a meeting at the very top. So they did something a bit weird. It

was well known that the founder and then-CEO of Southwest, the late Herb Kelleher, loved Wild Turkey whiskey. One of his famous quotes was, "Wild Turkey whiskey and Phillip Morris cigarettes are essential to the maintenance of human life!" (You're probably not going to hear anyone say that today . . . at least not publicly!) So they had an employee dress up in a turkey costume and run up and down the grass strip in front of Southwest's headquarters building in Texas. The ploy worked. They got a meeting with Kelleher. And Southwest became their client. I'm not recommending this as a bread-and-butter strategy for getting client meetings, but you never know.

In 1977, singer/songwriter Elvis Costello was struggling to get his early music recognized. So he parked himself in front of a hotel in London where CBS record executives were having a conference. As they exited the building at the end of the day, he began furiously playing short clips of his songs on his guitar, periodically shouting, "I'm Elvis Costello, sign me!" It worked.

Remember, however, that Costello had something to offer. His approach was unorthodox, but it was the value he was offering—the quality of his music—that drew in the CBS executives.

Often, it works to use multiple relationship-building techniques and touch points together. For example, one of my clients won a $10 million contract with a CEO who had never worked with them before. The first contact was through LinkedIn, when a managing director leveraged a mutual connection to get the CEO's attention. They invited the CEO to a high-profile firm event, which he attended. It turned out my client had an alliance with a well-known tech firm that the CEO already did business with, and that connection created more credibility. Face-to-face business discussions followed, leading to the deal.

My own successful strategy has been threefold. First, I maximize my relationships with current clients—I always try to super-serve them. Second, I attract prospects through my thought leadership and recognition as an authority in my field, using the strategies outlined in Week 2. And third, I get warm introductions to other senior executives I want to meet.

The more potential clients you get in front of, the more you'll be in the mix. It's a virtuous circle. The late, brilliant Jerry Panas was my coauthor for two of my books. He used to encourage the non-profits he advised to have *more* conversations with potential donors. Of course, many would say no. But some would end up making life-changing donations. Jerry used to say, "Some will. Some won't. So what?"

**PUTTING KEY IDEAS INTO ACTION**

To prioritize your client development investments, begin by segmenting your network. Create three tiers of contacts:

1. "A" List: Current and Past Clients
2. "B" List: VIP Contacts
3. "C" List: Other Contacts

### A. Current and Past Clients

- Make a list of all your current and past clients. First, prioritize current clients who are happy with your work and have additional needs you could meet, Then, list past satisfied clients.
- For existing clients, increase your understanding of their key priorities—go deeper into their strategy and future plans. Based on this, build or deepen your relationships with those specific

executives who can purchase the additional solutions you have in mind. Share examples of similar work you've done in those same areas for other clients.

- When you call past clients, your approach will vary depending on the strength of the relationship. For some, a simple "I was thinking about you and wanted to see how you are doing" may be sufficient to set up a call or meeting. For others, you may need to suggest a more specific agenda—"I know you've been investing to upgrade your risk management controls, and I had a couple of ideas I would like to share with you." If you have a good relationship with the person, it shouldn't be difficult to arrange a meeting. If you don't know him very well, then you may need a stronger "hook."

### B. VIP Contacts

These are your best relationships with influential individuals. As I mentioned earlier, they should be:

- Decision-makers at companies in your target market
- Individuals who can *introduce* you to or influence the decision-makers who buy your solutions
- People who, because of their experiences and connections, can *advise* you on how to penetrate a new client

Again, your approach to these VIP contacts will vary depending on the strength and longevity of the relationship. As you contact these people, your objectives are to deepen trust, understand their highest-priority issues, and build your credibility around your/your company's expertise and solutions.

## C. Other Contacts

You should go to this list only when you've exhausted current and past clients and your VIP contacts.

How many names should you have in each category? It totally depends on where you are in your career and in the development of your business. Current and Past Clients could be as few as 0 if you are just starting out, and as many as 50 or 100 executives (or more) if you're well into your career. VIP contacts could number from 5 to 100+. And you might have hundreds or thousands of people in the "Other Contacts" list.

These three tiers are summarized in Figure 3.2.

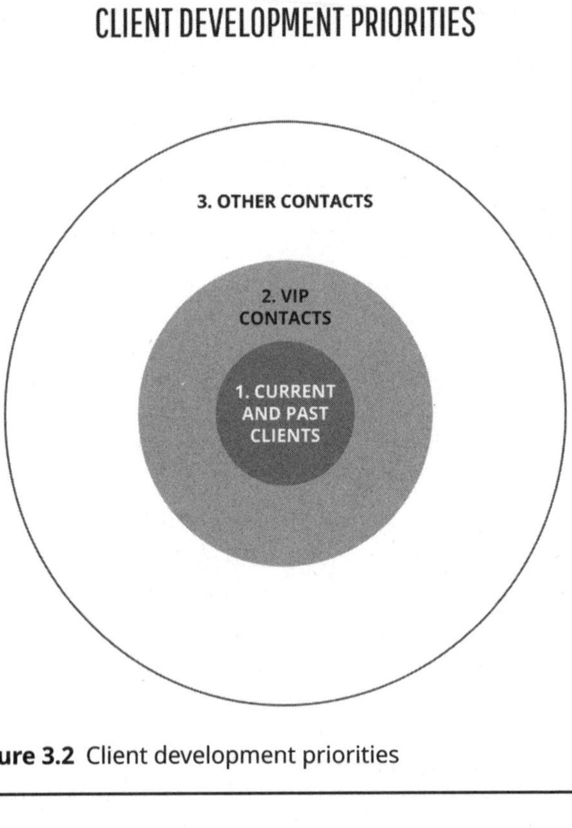


**Figure 3.2** Client development priorities

# Week 4 Master the First Meeting

The worst first meeting I ever had was with a senior vice president and two of his colleagues from a large telecommunications company. It was early in my career, but it was so bad I cringe even today when I think about it.

At the time I was still working with my old firm. We had a phenomenally successful business in the telecommunications industry, and I felt sure that the overwhelming weight of our experience would by itself bowl them over. I brought a beautiful deck of color 8x10 transparencies that I projected onto a big screen at the head of the conference room table (Does this date the meeting, just a little bit?). I gave a 45-minute, nonstop presentation on our capabilities, and then asked if there were any questions. They said no and fled the room in unison. Ouch!

Do I need to explain all the things I did wrong? I made a presentation instead of having a conversation. I talked nonstop at the client and didn't prepare thoughtful questions. I didn't add value that was specific to their challenges. Not surprisingly, I never heard from them again.

The second-worst meeting, which happened about 15 years ago, was with a large law firm. I met with two senior partners who seemed to have already made up their minds (in the negative). They peppered me nonstop with questions. I never gained my footing or turned the tide of the conversation. I ended up defensively responding to their pointed questions for about half an hour, and by then they were distracted and probably bored. The meeting lamely petered out.

Some first meetings just don't go well. But let's distinguish between an unforced error and a forced error. The first meeting I described was a train wreck because I blew it—it was an unforced error. The second meeting, with the law firm, was a forced error. I could have done better, but I walked into a buzz saw. It was never going to be a good meeting.

## The first meeting formula

Fortunately, I've also had hundreds of great first meetings. For these, I've followed a straightforward formula. It's simple, but requires studious practice. It goes like this: first, prepare—the *right* way. Then, when you meet, build rapport, establish your credibility, understand their issues, go deeper and add value in the conversation, and get a next step. I also endeavor to build trust, but this is done indirectly—I'll explain further on.

Last year, for example, I met for the first time with the chief client officer at a large company. We spent the first five minutes in small talk. I intentionally focused on some things we had in common in our background, and someone we both knew. I briefly described my practice. To do that, I didn't use any written material or slides. Rather, I shared an illustrative story about my work with an admired competitor, and some of the key lessons that emerged from it.

Then, I asked him three or four thoughtful questions about his most pressing issues. One of his challenges was right up my alley, and I provided examples of best practices I have seen for managing it. Later, I drew a graphic on the whiteboard in the room to help frame up the different options I felt he could consider. At the end of our hour, he enthusiastically suggested we schedule a follow-up conversation. Two weeks later, I had a signed contract.

If you had been watching, it would have looked like a very relaxed, engaging business conversation. It would not have come across as a sales pitch or a mechanical, orchestrated process.

How do we achieve this? Let's look in depth at each of these steps. Subsequently, in Weeks Five and Six, I'll go deeper into the process of turning a contact into a client, and I'll show you how to unlock a sale that has gotten stuck.

## Pre-meeting: Prepare smartly

Much of the preparation done for first meetings is well-meaning but *wrong*.

The first tendency is to get ready by doing lots of research on the company you're meeting with. I see people with background documents that are 100 or more pages long, stuffed with articles and annual reports. They weigh as much as a cinder block. And they are about as useful as one.

The second urge is to spend most of your time preparing and rehearsing your message—and, possibly, fine-tuning your presentation slides. Understandably, you want to be sure you can effectively communicate your points of view. You want to persuasively spell out the reasons why you and your firm are the best. But when you prepare too much, you get fixated on *your* message. You build in rigidity. The result is that you don't easily flex and improvise in the actual meeting.

Another problem with this kind of preparation is that it creates a high hurdle for you to have a meeting in the first place. It's a lot of work! In contrast, I want you to have *lots* of first meetings, both with new executives at existing clients and with prospects. Don't make it difficult by believing you need to spend hours and hours preparing for every business development conversation.

### Build in flexibility

Focus on lean, smart preparation. The best rainmakers I have studied do review the company's business. However, they spend much of their preparation time studying the *individual* they are going to meet. They invest to develop thoughtful questions that will engage their clients and draw them out.

Skim background material looking specifically for two things: facts about the company that stimulate an idea or "hook" you might use to engage the client, and things you want to ask questions about. What is the background and career history of the person you're meeting with? What can you learn about their personal style? The more you understand about them, the faster you will be able to build rapport when you meet.

President Abraham Lincoln was a master at this. He was famous for his deep empathy and uncanny ability to understand the temperament and motivations of others. He once said, "When I go to meet with a man, I spend one-third of my time thinking about what I am going to say, and two-thirds of my time thinking about what he is going to say."

### Bring two good ideas

Finally, always have two good ideas to share that you think might engage the executive. You want the first meeting (or for that matter the second or third meeting!) to be so engaging and value-added that the client is eager to have another conversation. Why two ideas (or more)? Because your first idea might fall flat, and you need a backup.

Believe me, it happens. I had a client who spent months trying to get a meeting with a high-value prospect. He and his team wanted to pitch the CEO of the company on an idea for using their software to enhance the customer experience. They banked everything on their concept. But in the first 10 minutes of the meeting, the CEO shot the idea down as old news. They had little else to say—no backup plan—and were unceremoniously ushered out when the CEO told them he suddenly had to run to another meeting.

Keep some of your powder dry. Always have a second idea in reserve.

**ANSWER THESE QUESTIONS**

Answer these questions as you prepare for your meeting:

- What challenges is this client's company/organization facing?
- What are the priorities, needs, and goals of the executive you're seeing?
- How can you help this client address these issues?
- What client examples will resonate with them?
- What is the other person like? What's her communications style? What do you have in common with him?
- What engaging, value-added ideas can you share?
- What are three, thought-provoking questions you'd like to ask?

## Objective one: Build rapport

A chief financial officer (CFO) told me that for over a decade he had refused to work with one particular investment bank. When he was a junior finance professional, a banker from this firm met him in a conference room to begin working on an acquisition. Without breaking the ice, and without asking, the banker grabbed the last ham sandwich sitting on a platter on the table. It happened to belong to the future CFO. The executive, with a straight face, said to me, "Never steal my lunch. It's a bad way to build rapport."

The banker had abysmally failed at two of the three key behaviors required to develop rapport.

### The three drivers of rapport

We all seem to know when we feel rapport with someone. But what exactly is it, and how can we increase it?

Rapport is a harmonious and sympathetic connection between you and the other person. There are two popular misconceptions about rapport. First, that some people are just born with natural charisma. This is not exactly true—you can *learn* to create a harmonious connection with people. And second, it's often taught that you can manipulate anyone into feeling rapport by using special techniques—like mirroring body language or engaging in behaviors known to stimulate oxytocin, a neuropeptide that may be associated with feelings of trust. Studies have shown, however, that if your efforts are insincere and manipulative, the other person usually sees right through them and trusts you *less.*

When we first meet someone in a professional setting, the amount of rapport we feel is based on our perception of three factors: Is he *trustworthy*? Is she *competent*? And, is the person *likable*?

*Driver number one: Are you trustworthy?*

When people meet you, they're wondering: Do you have my interests at heart, or are you here purely to pursue your own aims—or even to harm my interests? Their brains are asking, "Are you friend or foe?" Another term for this, used by researchers at Harvard, is "warmth."

These behaviors will accentuate your **trustworthiness** in a first conversation:

- Be warm and authentic. Use a friendly tone of voice, open body language, and good eye contact.
- Show an interest in the other person by asking good questions and listening deeply.
- Demonstrate integrity by being consistent, reliable, and straightforward. Don't exaggerate. Align your body language and speech.
- Affirm and synthesize as you listen. You can use interjections such as *uh-huh*, *ok*, and *I see* to show you're listening, but don't overdo it. These are especially important when you're on the phone, to reassure the other person you're still there.
- Don't be afraid to talk earnestly about your passions and interests, and why you do what you do—this conveys warmth and authenticity.

Some people have tried to reduce the trust-building process down to the simple manipulation of the above-mentioned chemical, oxytocin. This strategy is the subject of one of the most popular TED talks ever given, as well as a book on trust. The problem is, many scientists now believe the research these pundits relied on was faulty. One article in *Vox* is entitled, "How Scientists Fell in and out of Love with the Hormone Oxytocin." Oh—and the main technique for getting the other person's brain to produce oxytocin and trust you? Eight hugs a day. One promoter of the oxytocin theory reputedly give lots of hugs to people when he meets them. If you're talking about your spouse or partner, I'm all for hugs. But in a professional setting? Really?

Stick to proven, professional behaviors that we know, from both experience and research studies, will build trust.

### *Driver number two: Are you competent?*

The second factor that drives rapport is perceived **competence**. In a professional setting, people are evaluating whether you know what you're talking about. Can you deliver?

You demonstrate you are competent when you:

- Exhibit professionalism, which includes appropriate dress, grooming, etiquette, and the right balance of formal/informal speech (e.g., say "Does your organization . . ." instead of "Do you guys . . ." etc.).
- Communicate confidently and clearly. State your point and pause—don't use filler words such as *like*, *you know*, *uh-huh*, *kinda*, and so on. Tape yourself in a conversation and review it afterwards—it's a great way to make your speech crisper. (Do tell the other person you're recording!)
- Ask questions that inherently demonstrate your knowledge of the issues, e.g., "Some of my clients are rapidly moving to employ blended learning experiences that combine eLearning, classroom training, and small group work. What is *your* current learning and development approach?" But don't ask questions to show off and look clever, which will make your client cringe.
- Share thoughtful points of view, perspectives, and ideas for dealing with the client's problems and opportunities.

*Driver number three: Are you likable?*

The third factor is **likability**. We want to engage with people we like, and when we like someone, we feel at ease with them and more open to a relationship.

Clients often tell me the following when I interview them about their most trusted relationships: "I don't work with jerks. I work with people I like."

Your likability will increase when you:

- Find commonalities and similarities. If the other person feels he has something in common with you, it immediately drives up your likability.
- Exude energy and enthusiasm. Research shows that a high level of enthusiasm is a very likable quality.
- Be human and accessible—confident but also humble.
- Ask emotional/personal questions ("Of all the initiatives you have underway, what are you personally most excited about?")
- Walk in thinking, "I like this person." When the other person perceives that you like her, your *own* likability goes up.
- Focus on the other person, as opposed to talking extensively about yourself. Synthesize what you've heard and repeat it back. Before instantly blurting out your next response, pause for a few seconds to show you've listened and are considering what they've said.

## Define the agenda

Before you move to objective number two, you also need to define the agenda for the meeting. This is not a housekeeping item—it's part of establishing a collaborative, peer relationship with the other person. It also demonstrates confidence.

Here are some conversational techniques I use to do this:

*General approach:* "I understand we've got one hour scheduled for this discussion—is that right? (pause) I wanted to share with you my approach to building clients for life and describe a couple of examples of how I've helped other firms improve both their new client acquisition and their ability to grow and retain existing relationships. Then, I'd love to hear about your efforts to grow your client base and what your most important priorities are right now. At the end of our conversation, I'm sure we'll both have a good sense for whether or not it makes sense to continue the dialogue. Is there anything else that you'd like to make sure we cover?"

*Open approach* (either they requested the meeting, or you want to invite them to define exactly what they want to focus on): "I understand we've got about 45 minutes today. From your perspective, what would be the most valuable way for us to use this time?" (*Note:* This can be a very powerful way to get the client to "reach" and tell you *exactly* what they want to get out of the discussion.)

*Topic-specific approach* (e.g., the client has previously been very specific about what they want to focus on): "I understand from our email exchange that you'd like to increase the ability of your people to act as strategic advisors to their clients. Let me start by asking you to say more about that issue—for example, for you, what does it mean to be a strategic advisor, and what's the gap you've identified? Later, if it would be useful, I can share some examples of projects I've done for other clients to help them significantly improve the trusted advisor skills of their client service partners."

## Objective two: Establish your credibility

The CEO of a mid-sized technology company told me he received a call from a very well-known management consulting firm. He didn't know the partner, but some quick research revealed an impressive background. Because of this, and the firm's excellent reputation, he agreed to meet. In addition, he was pondering some changes to his strategy, and he figured he might learn something from a conversation with this firm.

After exchanging pleasantries, the partner and a colleague sat down on the sofa in the CEO's office. The partner leaned back, and said, "So, tell us a bit about your business. What are the toughest issues you're facing right now?"

The CEO, annoyed and frustrated, replied, "No. I'm not going to share that with you right off the bat. First, tell me why you are here and what the agenda is. Then, add some value in the conversation. After that, maybe I'll share what I'm thinking."

The point is that unless you are already well known to the client you are meeting with, you have to build your credibility. You can't just plop down and start peppering the client with questions. But here's the catch: You must learn how to build your credibility in about three or four minutes. Otherwise, you will make the conversation too much about you and not enough about your prospective client. You also need do it *indirectly.* When you try to say "I'm smart and experienced," it's not believable. Of course you'd say you are!

Don't rely on a slide deck or brochure to make yourself credible. Clients want to have a conversation, not be presented to. You might bring a few slides as a leave-behind, but not as the main meal. Better idea: if you have frameworks or diagrams you want to show, draw them on a flip chart or whiteboard. It's called "pencil selling" and it's far more engaging than projecting a slide.

The first way you demonstrate credibility is by showing up ready to have a productive conversation. This is where your smart preparation comes in. Amazingly, many clients have told me pathetic stories about professionals, from well-known firms, who arrive knowing almost nothing about the client's business.

Being prepared is table stakes. Here are three additional, powerful ways to indirectly establish your credibility in a believable, authentic manner.

### One: Share value-added points of view (POV)

A point of view is a brief statement, possibly a provocative one, about how you see an important trend developing that is affecting your client. It could be about the industry, customers, competition, a functional area, the economy—you name it. Your point of view should be 50 to 150 words in length. In other words, it should take you about a minute or less to convey.

The great management thinker and author Peter Drucker was brilliant at conveying penetrating points of view in just a sentence or two. He is famous for expressions such as "Management is doing things right; leadership is doing the right things" and "Most of what we call management consists of making it difficult for people to get their work done."

### Two: Ask credibility-building questions

These are questions which inherently demonstrate your knowledge and experience. You make a statement, and then flip it into a question.

For example, I might say, "It sounds like gaining more collaboration to serve your clients across organizational silos is an issue for you. In looking at my other clients, the three most common barriers to collaboration I see are . . . (then I list them). But I'm curious, in your own organization what particular obstacles are getting in the way?"

These are not the *only* type of questions you should ask. As I've mentioned, you should spend significant prep time developing three thought-provoking questions for every meeting. In Week 10 of this plan, I'll go into greater depth about how to use powerful questions with your clients.

### Three: Use client examples—"What we finds"

While living in London, I once had a particularly high-profile meeting with the head of strategic planning for a large corporation. Over the course of an hour, I just couldn't find an issue that energized and engaged the client. The meeting ended, and I glumly departed. I suddenly stopped in the doorway, however, and leaned back into his office. "You know, there's one other example of work we have done that you might be interested in." It was a desperate, "Hail Mary" play, but I hated leaving empty-handed. I quickly shared a high-impact project we had done for a competitor, in an area I was not particularly expert in at all—information technology (which is probably why I hadn't used that example!). The client nodded, and again thanked me for my time. Three days later he called me back to hear more about this example, and three months later they bought a $2 million project that ultimately turned into a $4 million a year relationship (today, equivalent to around $8 million). I trace it back, 100%, to my having gone to school on client examples.

Client examples—like a point of view—should very brief. These are not long case studies. They are conversational. Don't tell your prospect all the details. Instead, focus on three things: the original problem the client wanted to solve; the approach you took (which ideally illustrates the *uniqueness* of your solution); and the results or impact.

Write down your examples, hone and polish them. Practice speaking them out loud. Record them and listen to how they sound. Memorize them—if you don't, instead of giving a crisp, one-minute example you will spend five minutes wandering through your case study, which will surely stultify the client. If they want to hear more, they'll ask!

Finally, make sure you have permission to give the name of the company and the executive you worked with. This adds heft and believability to the example. If you don't have permission, then disguise the example.

## Objective three: Understand their issues

By five to eight minutes into your meeting, you should have built some rapport, established the agenda for your conversation, and built your credibility using the techniques outlined above. Then, you should flip the attention from you to your client. You need to draw them into the conversation and explore their issues.

Every meeting is different. For some, you will have very little idea about what the client is truly concerned about. In that case, based on your pre-meeting preparation, you will ask a few questions designed to tease out their issues. Say you're talking to a chief human resources officer (CHRO)—a good start might be, "I understand you're undergoing a major strategy shift right now and reorganizing around industry sectors. How is that impacting your priorities for HR?"

For others, they will have specified exactly what they want to discuss. Your question to a chief financial officer (CFO) may be simply, "You mentioned that you're transforming your approach to risk management—can you say more about that initiative?"

Your objective, in every case, is to identify an issue that you and the client can productively engage around.

Strive to uncover a challenge that one of your solutions can solve.

I can't emphasize enough the importance of searching for that singular, urgent issue you can build the rest of your sales process around. You must be patient, because it may very well take two or even three meetings to get there. But it's worth it. As you'll see in Week 6, if there's no urgent issue that the client cares about, there's no sale.

## Objective four: Go deep and add value

At this point, you are now about 15 or 20 minutes into your meeting. If have been able to identify an important issue that you might help the client with, then the next 20 minutes or so should be spent exploring that issue. In Week 8, I'll share some very specific techniques and questions for exploring an issue and reframing it. In the meantime, here are some quick tips for what should come next.

I use a simple paradigm to understand the scope and gravity of virtually any issue. It goes like this:

1. What are your aspirations and goals for X? (X = the business or area that is under discussion.) What do you want your business/this area to look like in two to three years? What level of performance do you want to see?
2. What is the gap between the capabilities you have today and the ones you need to support your aspirations—the future state you aspire to? Put another way, what is stopping you or getting in your way?
3. What capabilities do you need to develop to bridge this gap? Let's say I'm talking to a company that wants to move from being a vendor to acting as a trusted partner to their clients. Here are some actual conversation samples from my dialogue:

> **YOUR SECRET WEAPON: EVOKE THEIR CURIOSITY**
>
> Years ago, one of my mentors, Alan Weiss, said to me: "Andrew, you're extremely knowledgeable, but remember, tell people what they need to know, not *everything* you know!" Funny, but good advice.
>
> Another important maxim I've found invaluable is, "Leave them wanting more." Whether it's your first or fifth meeting, you want to leave the other person curious to learn more, not overwhelmed at all the information you have sprayed at them through a high-pressure fire hose.
>
> Evoke their curiosity by mentioning new information and insights that you can discuss during your next meeting, suggesting another client you'd like them to meet, or perhaps offering to interview other members of their team to in turn present a point of view on their challenge.

- "Can you say more about what it would mean to be a trusted partner to your clients? What would that relationship look like?"
- "What changes would you expect to see in your financial results—revenue growth, profitability, cost of sales, and so on?"
- "You mentioned to me that you have around 500 clients. How many would you say are currently in the 'trusted partner' category?"
- "So if today that number is only 5%, what would you hope it would be in three years?"
- "What are some of the barriers that get in the way of building these valuable, trusted-partner relationships?"
- "What kinds of capabilities do you feel you need to put in place—people, skills, systems, and so on—in order to reach your goal of having a trusted partner relationship with 35% of your clients?"
- "What percentage of your current client-facing professionals are capable today of building these types of relationships? And what percentage of those who are *not* capable today do you think could be trained and coached to do it?"

You get the idea.

When I say you need to *add value* in the conversation, I mean that you need to sharpen the client's understanding of their problem or opportunity. This could include educating them about how others have solved their challenges, making them aware of the solutions that exist, and giving them concrete ideas for tackling the issue. It could also mean being very direct about what you believe will work and not work for them. A further way to make the conversation highly engaging is to pose some thought-provoking questions the client hasn't been asked before.

There are many ways of "adding value" in a business development meeting. In Week 13 I'll give you some proven strategies for how to add what I call *value for time.*

## Objective five: Get a next step

It's an old adage that the goal of every first meeting is to get a second meeting. If you've built initial trust and rapport, and added value in the conversation, there's a good chance you'll earn a second shot.

There are two main strategies you can pursue. The first is to briefly summarize the discussion and proactively suggest a next step. This could be another conversation to go deeper, or something else, like meeting other executives in the organization. I usually try to offer something of value to encourage further dialogue. For example: "Would it be helpful if I put together a one-page outline of how I would approach this challenge? Then we could meet again next week to discuss it." Or "Is this the right issue we should focus on as we take this conversation forward?"

This is akin to a "trial close." A trial close is when you ask a question in order to determine where you are in the sales process and ascertain the strength of the buyer's commitment.

The second option is to invite the client to suggest a next step. I usually do this when I want the other person to reach toward me. The best buyer is willing and enthusiastic. If I don't sense much interest or commitment, then I will summarize the key issues we've discussed and simply ask: "So, from your perspective, what would a good next step be?" I like this approach because it forces the client's hand. They either have to say, yes, I want a next step; or no, I don't think it makes sense to talk more about this right now.

I use option one about 75% of the time, and option two around 25% of the time.

Of course, it's possible the next step is to write a proposal. But, especially for a complex sale, that would be very unlikely after just one meeting—especially if it's with a new prospect.

Figure 4.1 summarizes these five steps.

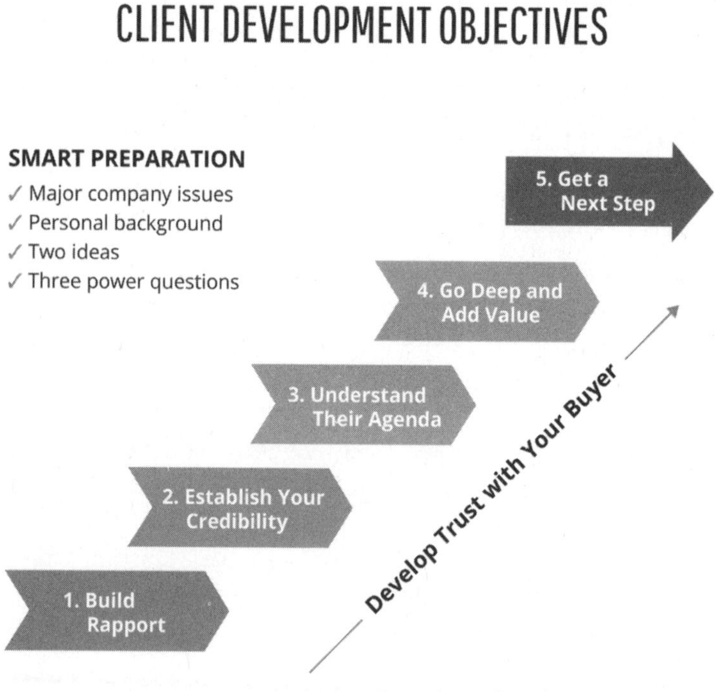


**Figure 4.1** Client development objectives

## What clients say about first meetings

I've interviewed thousands of C-suite executives, and I always ask about first meetings. In conducting my research, I use questions such as: "Can you give me your perspective on first meetings? When an external provider walks into your office for the first time, what works well? What builds trust and credibility and makes you interested in pursuing the relationship? What are your pet peeves about first meetings—what mistakes do people make?"

Don't take it from me—read these typical comments from senior executives. They speak for themselves:

- "If you send me an email requesting a meeting, add specificity to your message. Talk about how you can add value to my business and help me with a key initiative, not all the details of your product or service."
- "Show me how your solution can help solve a challenge I have. Don't go on and on about how great your product is—talk about how you can help me. Share how you've worked with other companies like mine on similar problems."
- "You have to come prepared, which means knowing the basics of my business and what our issues are. You'd be surprised how many people walk in here knowing almost nothing about me or my company."
- "If we're meeting for the first time, don't act like you're my buddy. Being overly familiar is a real turnoff."
- "Don't sell in your first meeting. It's an exploratory conversation. Don't start pressing me to buy something!"
- "Don't ask for a meeting with me and then arrive and start peppering me with questions right off the bat. Explain why you're here and what the objective is. Show me some credibility and add value. You can then ask questions later in the discussion."

- "Don't present to me. It's boring. I want to have a conversation, not read slides."
- "Learn as much as you can about my agenda before you arrive. But that said, don't presume to know what's really on my mind—don't walk in and inform me of what my issues are."

Should you always pursue these five objectives, in this order, in all of your first meetings? In Week 5, "From Contact to Contract," I'll delve into this question. The short answer is: No. What I've just described is your foundational template for a great business development conversation. But, depending on the type of meeting it is, you'll make some small but very strategic changes in the process I just described.

### PUTTING KEY IDEAS INTO ACTION

In my introduction on Day 1, I talked about making a powerful shift from the expert or product mindset to the *advisor* mindset. Below, I've listed *advisor* behaviors you should adopt and *expert* behaviors you must avoid in order to succeed at the five objectives I've just outlined.

#### Practice these advisor behaviors

- Find commonalities and similarities.
- Be curious about your client *as a person.*
- Set the agenda: Why are you there?
- Walk in confidently, as a peer (without being arrogant).
- "Show" by using engaging client examples.
- Have a conversation and use a whiteboard or flipchart if appropriate (use slides only as a leave-behind).

- Establish your credibility indirectly, with credibility-building questions.
- Ask implication questions about the impact of key changes and trends.
- Ask questions about their business that show you've prepared for the meeting.
- Ask about their aspirations and the gap between the present and future state.
- Share best practices and what other companies are doing.
- Remember to allocate five or 10 minutes to summarize your conversation and discuss next steps.
- Evoke their curiosity by suggesting something of value you can subsequently share.

**Avoid these expert behaviors**

- Undervalue the need to build rapport and minimize or skip this step altogether.
- Fail to go beyond superficial talk (the weather) and really connect.
- Walk in as a subordinate, not a peer.
- "Tell" by using data and formal credentials ("We have five offices . . .").
- Use a slide deck or brochure in a first meeting.
- Go into excessive detail about your methodologies.
- Ask stale, clichéd questions like, "What keeps you up at night?"
- Ask more than a few closed-ended questions ("What's your market share?").
- Spend too much time describing your solutions.
- Wait until the meeting is virtually over to discuss next steps.
- Offer to write a proposal without having laid the proper foundations for the sale.

**ADDITIONAL FREE RESOURCES FOR YOU**

Download my free *Client Growth Guide* at www.andrewsobel.com/growth-guide. It includes the checklists, First Meeting Pitfalls and Holding Great Executive Meetings, as well as dozens of other practical strategies and tools for growing your client base.

# Week 5 From Contact to Contract

Shortly after writing my first book, *Clients for Life*, I got a call from the head of training at a fast-growing Fortune 500 company. Her CEO had read my book and liked the approach. He asked her to contact me to explore opportunities to work together.

We had several good conversations. I shared a great deal of information about how her company could become more client-centric and the practices that would help their account executives grow their client relationships.

When she asked me how much I would charge for a workshop, however, everything went south. There was a long silence on the telephone after I named the fee. "We just couldn't afford that," she finally replied. In retrospect, I should have insisted on talking to the CEO earlier in the process, but—well, this was nearly 20 years ago, and I've learned a few things since then. I stuck to my guns, however, and didn't budge on the fee. For the time being, that was the end of it.

Holding firm turned out to be the right strategy. The first opportunity that was presented to me wasn't the right one.

One year later, the head of training called me again. "Andrew, I believe now is the right time to involve you. We have the right event, and the budget to afford you." I was invited to speak at the annual conference of their top 500 executives from around the world. This launched a relationship that has endured to this day. It's been one of my best and largest clients, year after year, and the CEO has been an enthusiastic supporter of my work.

There was a bit of providence involved as well. That company continued to grow year after year, becoming the leader in its sector. It became especially noted for its high levels of client service and low client turnover.

The point here is simple: I want you to win the sale, but just as importantly I want you to *win the client.* Sometimes, the client just isn't ready to buy from you. And sometimes, it's not the right deal for you. When this happens, I want you to make such a good impression during the sales process—to add so much value—that you get a second chance further down the road.

During this week's challenge, you're going to learn five additional, important strategies for winning both the sale *and* the client.

## Two simple rules to sequence your sales conversations

In Week 4, I outlined the five objectives for a first meeting. The sequencing and emphasis on these objectives, however, will vary depending on several important factors.

I hear a lot of black-and-white proclamations about how to run a business development conversation. "Start out your meeting by asking lots of questions so that you get the client talking" is a common truism. Or—and this one is in several popular books on selling—"The client should talk 80% of the time and you should talk only 20% of the time." That's like saying all keynote speeches must be 30 minutes long, which is ridiculous. Sometimes, it's appropriate for the client to speak 80% of the time, but under other circumstances, the balance may be more like 50–50.

The first big variable that determines the order of your agenda is whether *you* asked for the meeting or the *client* asked for the meeting. A second important variable is whether the meeting is with a new prospect or with an executive at an existing client. The matrix, shown in Figure 5.1, illustrates how you need to adapt the flow of your conversation.

## FOUR TYPES OF CLIENT DEVELOPMENT CONVERSATIONS

| | Existing Client | Prospective Client |
|---|---|---|
| **You Asked for the Meeting** | **ADVOCATE**<br>1. Share value-added observations about their organization and issues<br>2. Get their reaction, ask questions, and explore the issue with them | **ADVOCATE**<br>1. Develop rapport, set the agenda, and build your credibility<br>2. Then explore their issues with agenda-setting questions |
| **They Asked for the Meeting** | **INQUIRE**<br>1. First, listen<br>2. Ask questions to explore the issue<br>3. Share relevant examples and ideas, and engage in initial problem solving | **INQUIRE**<br>1. First, listen<br>2. Ask questions to explore the issue<br>3. Build your credibility with client examples and value-added perspectives |

**Figure 5.1** Four types of client development conversations

In other words: If the client has asked for the meeting, you can generally kick off by asking questions about why they wanted to see you and the issue they have presented. But if *you* asked for the meeting, you need to set up the agenda. And, if it's with a brand-new prospect, you've got to go through the credibility-building steps I outlined in Week 4, "Master the First Meeting."

It's a painful sight watching someone robotically move through a presentation and ignore all the signals they are getting from the client. So use the five objectives and the techniques I've shared with you in a modular fashion. Be flexible, and mix and match them depending on the circumstances.

## Identifying and managing the key stakeholders

A large consulting firm I advised learned the hard way how important stakeholder alignment is. They had invested $250,000 in a huge proposal to a Fortune 100 company, working with the COO (chief operating officer). At the final presentation, the chairman of the company unexpectedly showed up. The COO had assured them the chairman was not going to be involved in the decision. However, it turned out that he had a significant personal shareholding in the company, and was very influential with the board of directors. His opinions were infrequently offered but carried heavy weight.

When my client finished the pitch, the chairman jumped out of his chair and said, "There's absolutely no justification to pay an outside firm to perform this work. Our own people should be doing it." And then he unceremoniously left the room. Needless to say, the project was scratched by the very apologetic COO.

If you are selling your products or services to corporations, you will invariably have to deal with a variety of stakeholders in the sales process. If you ignore important influencers, you may very well shoot yourself in the foot. You'll invest in writing a proposal, but get shot down because you didn't bother to cultivate support from the main decision-maker and other important executives. Even if you are talking to a CEO, who can unilaterally make a decision to buy from you, it's likely you'll need to get other executives on board.

Here are the main types of stakeholders or "influencers" you need to identify and win over:

**TREAT PROSPECTS LIKE CLIENTS AND THEY'LL LIKELY BECOME ONE**

I once interviewed a CEO who told me about a supplier that had sought their business. "They doggedly met with us," he told me, "even though we told them there was no way we were going to buy from them. Each time, however, they shared strong insights about our business. After a year, my people said to me, 'They are adding more value to us than our current supplier.' We hired them."

You have to be prudent about where you invest your time. But I don't really distinguish between a "prospect" and a "client" when I'm having a business conversation—I try to act as a trusted advisor to everyone I meet with. I generously share my knowledge. I tell them what I would do if I owned the business. I'm enthusiastic and I enjoy the conversation, and it shows.

- **Decision-Maker.** This is the person who can make the decision to buy from you, *without* getting approval from others. *A decision-maker is asking, "Is this a good investment for my organization—will it have a high ROI? Do you have the right capabilities to meet our needs?"*
- **Day-to-Day Buyer.** This is the individual who will work with you on a day-to-day basis. He or she can't make the final decision about your proposal—that would be the decision-maker—but this person is

often very influential. Sometimes, the decision-maker is also the day-to-day buyer.

*This buyer is asking, "Can we work well together? Will you help me achieve my goals?"*

- **Feasibility Buyer.** This is someone who has been assigned to identify and scope out possible suppliers. I don't like dealing with them, because they can say "No" but not "Yes"! They will often press you for a proposal or price quote. Don't get sucked in! You'll usually waste your time if you send them a proposal after one meeting or phone call. Make friends with this person, and learn as much as you can about the company's challenges. But insist on meeting the decision-maker.

  *The feasibility buyer wants to know, "Do you meet our requirements? Can I put you forward as a valid option?"*
- **Procurement Buyer.** Procurement is a fact of life. The best procurement executives are genuinely looking for the ideal combination of attributes—price, value, quality, service, etc.—to meet the needs of the business. The worst ones just want to get you to cut your price, so they can say they did their job and saved the company money.

  *Procurement buyers want to ascertain whether you have met the requirements to be a vendor to their company. Usually, they want to know if your price is the lowest.*
- **Other Influencers.** These are usually other executives whose departments or functions will be impacted by the purchase, and/or who can often invisibly exercise influence over a buying decision. The chairman who crashed the sale at the last minute, in my story at the beginning of this section, was a good example of one. He was a powerful influencer who didn't fit neatly into the previously listed categories.

Your goal is to identify and win over all the key stakeholders in the process. You should meet them, understand what they are looking for, and build trust. They must be convinced you are the best, highest-value alternative (versus doing it internally), and that their own personal goals will be respected and aided. The larger the contract, the more stakeholders there will usually be.

There's one additional stakeholder—"role" is perhaps a better term—that was highlighted years ago by the authors Miller and Heiman in their book *Strategic Selling*. This is the *coach*. A coach is someone who has insider knowledge of the client's organization and wants to help you win the sale. A coach could be the decision-maker, a junior manager, or even a former employee. They help you navigate the organization, understand the needs of the different influencers, and develop the right strategy to succeed. For any sort of complex sale, you need a coach. If you don't have one, you are at a disadvantage.

## Moving from contact to contract

I've had sales cycles that lasted one hour. I've also had sales that took a year. What exactly is the magical tipping point when a good conversation transforms into a sold proposal? In the broadest terms, a sale happens when the client trusts you and believes your solution is the best option to help them fix an important problem or capture an attractive opportunity.

There are two important dimensions that underpin this shift from talk to action: the process of building trust, and an understanding of the rational, political, and personal elements of the sale.

## How to rapidly build trust

An executive I know proposed an idea for a new project to one of his clients. He was rebuffed. The client told him, "You know, it feels a bit like you guys are just trying to sell us something here." My friend's solution was to revamp the proposal and try to make it more appealing to the client.

I told him the real problem wasn't the proposal—rather, it was a lack of trust in the relationship. He looked at me, quite surprised. I explained the issue: "Look," I told him, "if your client really trusted you, when you brought him a proposal he would be fully confident you were only doing so in his company's best interests. And he would never say you were just trying to get a sale!"

Over the next five months my friend spent more face-time with his client, got to know him better, and focused on adding value to one of his key challenges. The client's trust in him grew, and the proposal was later accepted.

Trust is both the universal lubricant and glue of relationships. It reduces the inevitable frictions inherent in working with others. It enables the creation of deep, resilient connections at work and at home. Social scientists say that trust improves virtually every aspect of the human experience.

The formal definition of trust is "the assured reliance on the character, ability, strength, or truth of someone or something." Put more simply, it's the feeling that the other person will meet our expectations of them. How do we develop a client's trust in us? It boils down to five key factors, illustrated in Figure 5.2.

First, clients need to believe you are *competent* at what you do—that you can deliver on your promises. Competence-based trust will go up or down depending on what someone is asking you to do. A client may trust you to streamline their accounting process, but not to develop their business strategy. You may trust a plumber to fix your leaky faucet, but not to paint your walls. So

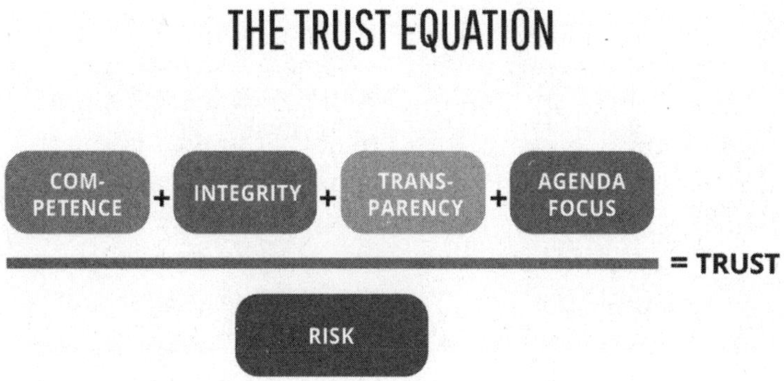


**Figure 5.2** The trust equation

part of the challenge is influencing the client's *perception* of your competence in different areas.

Second, trust is based on *integrity*. Remember the term "integer" from math? It means a whole number. When you have integrity, you are an integral "whole" of consistent values, beliefs, and behaviors. Having integrity means being honest, of course, but it's more than that. It also means being consistent, reliable, and discreet.

The third factor that builds trust is *transparency*. Have you heard the expression, used to describe someone, "What you see is what you get." In other words, they don't have secrets or hidden agendas—they are open and share information with you. Conversely, when a client feels you are not communicating, or worse, being evasive, trust plummets.

One client of mine told me about a law firm he had used for many years. Their lawyers made a mistake on a legal document. It was quite serious, but apparently it would not have been noticed for a year or two. The law firm, when they realized the error, immediately drew it to his attention. He told me he then trusted them *more*, not less, because of their honesty and openness in reporting the error. "I know you'll always be forthcoming with me," he told them.

The fourth trust ingredient is *agenda focus* or intent. Are you focused on the client's agenda—on their interests and how you can help them? Or are you working your own agenda? When you feel the other person is suggesting something that he insists is in your best interests, but which is really in *his* best interests, it's a serious red flag.

Finally, the last ingredient is *perceived risk.* Approving a contract for a $50 million IT investment is a far riskier proposition than placing an order to buy office supplies, and the standard of trust is naturally much higher. As perceived risk goes down, trust rises. Your challenge: takes steps to reduce your client's perception of the risk of buying from you.

Here are some behaviors that will help you build trust with clients:

- *Meet all commitments.* Be extraordinarily reliable, and treat the smallest commitment with the same gravity you treat a major one. Respond rapidly. Always be on time. If clients can't trust you to come through for a small thing, why would they trust you with something large and important?
- *Always maintain confidences.* Build a reputation as someone who is discreet and never criticizes people who are not in the room.
- *Be candid and forthright.* Answer clients' questions honestly and forthrightly. If necessary, say, "I don't know—but I'll get an answer for you tomorrow."
- *Communicate often.* Your clients' trust in you and perception of delivered value will usually rise with the frequency and quality of your communications.
- *Do things that are clearly in the clients' interests but not in yours.* If clients see you definitively putting their needs first, it bolsters their trust in you.
- *Spend time together.* Face-time builds likability and familiarity, which enhances trust. *Helpful:* organize

opportunities to see your client outside the office. By changing the relationship environment, you deepen the connection (e.g., have lunch outside the office, invite your client to a conference, and so on).

- *Reduce your client's perception of risk.* Have a prospect talk to an existing client who can testify to the results you helped them achieve. Break a contract down into discrete chunks, with checkpoints along the way. Guarantee the quality of your work (but not necessarily the specific outcomes. These are largely outside your control, as they depend greatly on the client's own leadership and implementation effectiveness).

## Manage the rational, political, and personal

Early in my career, a client asked my firm to assess how to restore one of his business units to profitability. The government had a major stake in his company. Our analysis showed there was significant potential in the business, but it would require a large investment to realize it. To me and my team, it made complete sense to proceed with the restructuring—it was the rational decision.

When I presented our recommendations to my client, however, he was taken aback. He said there was no way he could proceed. The rational case gave a green light to invest more money into the company to restore it to health. But we had ignored the political and personal considerations. The large consulting project we were suggesting could potentially put my client at significant personal risk. His goal was to survive his tenure as CEO unscathed, without any scandals or financial disasters. His goal, and the government's as well, was risk management, not growth. Spending a lot of money on outside consultants also exposed him to being attacked by the government for wasting taxpayers' money.

Had we considered all three dimensions, we would have come up with a smaller project design that made more sense and met the client's objectives.

If you are proposing a major transaction to a client, here are some questions you should ask yourself about each of these three factors:

## Rational

- What are the rational arguments for the client to buy your product or service?
- How will your solution help your client's organization meet its strategic, operational, and financial goals?
- What will the quantifiable value and impact be (e.g., increased revenue and profits, reduced costs, etc.)? What will the qualitative benefits be (e.g., improved culture, greater teamwork, etc.)?

## Political

- How will working with you/your firm affect your client's standing and relationships within her organization?
- What are the different goals of the other stakeholders across the client's enterprise? How might your proposal affect them, and how will they react to it?

## Personal

- How does your proposal support or tie into the *personal* aspirations and desires of the key buying influences? For example: goals concerning their career, learning agenda, networking, personal development, personal performance objectives for the year, and so on.

Failing to take into account all three of these factors is like doing surgery without monitoring a patient's blood pressure, respiration, and heart rate. Figure 5.3 summarizes these three levels.

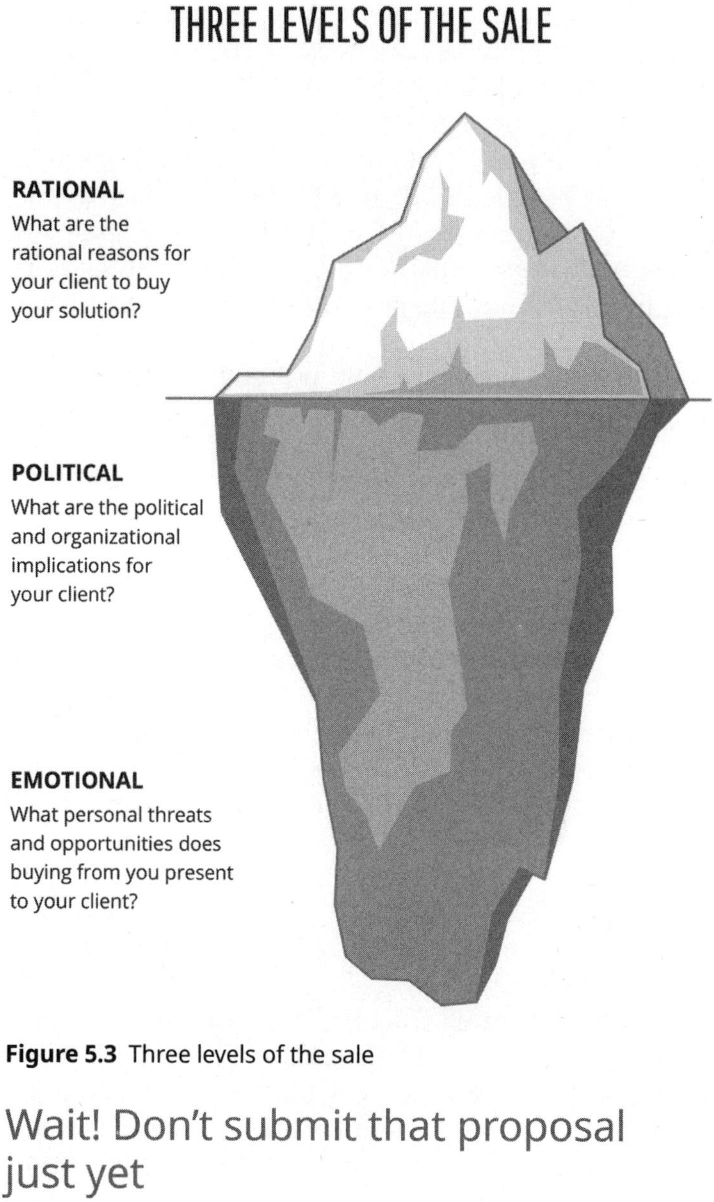


**Figure 5.3** Three levels of the sale

## Wait! Don't submit that proposal just yet

Writing a good proposal is a big investment. It usually requires ample amounts of both time and money. A company could easily spend 10% of revenues on sales, and a lot of that gets put into developing proposals. Unfortunately, many proposals fail because they are submitted too soon, or should not even have been written in the first place. Others sub-optimize the opportunity, which I'll talk about in Week 8, "Reframe for Maximum Impact."

In my experience, there are large, untapped opportunities to increase your ROI and improve your proposal win rate. I have seen many of my clients do this by skipping the least promising proposal opportunities and then doubling down on the highest potential ones.

You need to confirm eight preconditions before you write and submit a proposal:

1. **It is the right client and the right issue.** Is this an appropriate client, given your strategy? For example, is it the right size, in the right industry, in the right geographic area, and so on? Is this issue in your "sweet spot" in terms of capabilities? Is the executive with whom you will work an effective, respected individual in their organization?
2. **The issue has been clearly defined.** You must have a thorough understanding of the issue or issues you are being asked to address. This could happen in one conversation, but more likely will only unfold over two or three meetings. Remember: Sometimes clients haven't actually defined the issue very well. And their articulation of it may change over the course of several meetings.
3. **You have framed the totality of the problem and of the solution.** Clients often define their problem too narrowly. Your job is to diplomatically explore all aspects of the issue in order to recommend the best solution. In Week 8 we'll take a deep dive into reframing strategies.
4. **You and the client are in agreement about the value and impact of the proposed work.** It's essential to learn what is most important to the client.

What particular value are they seeking? Is speed critical? How important is cost? What about quality? You need to have explored the quantitative and qualitative impact that the client envisions, and have their signoff on that value case.

5. **You understand the client's buying process.** Do you know how your client is going to make a decision, who will be involved, what the selection criteria are, and what their timeframe is? It is completely appropriate to ask questions such as: "Can you walk me through your decision-making process and timeframe? Who are the major stakeholders who need to be aligned before you can go forward? Who will make the final decision about selecting a firm to work with?"
6. **You have met with the decision-maker or executive sponsor.** Sometimes this person is also referred to as the *economic buyer.* You need to speak to and, ideally, meet the person who is the overall executive sponsor of the initiative. This is the executive who will make the final decision to hire you or someone else. If you haven't met the person, you are flying blind because you won't know what his or her specific objectives and expectations are. Besides, people buy from people they like and trust . . . and if you haven't met, they will lack the most powerful reasons for choosing you!
7. **You and the client have reached conceptual agreement about the proposal.** You must have discussed the essential elements of your proposal with the client and reached a high-level agreement about it before you submit it. You might say, "Before I send you this proposal, I'd like to meet with you to walk through our basic approach. That way I can get your reactions and input before finalizing it." If you don't have this conceptual approval, you are at risk of turning in a proposal that is not quite on target and/or will get picked apart by the client.

8. **You have scheduled a follow-up discussion to review the proposal and the client's reaction to it.** Make an agreement with the client to discuss the proposal after you submit it. Schedule a phone call or face-to-face meeting to ensure the client's commitment to read the proposal and share his or her reactions with you.

---

Think about the proposals you have written where three or four of these preconditions were not met. What was your success rate? How about proposals where all of these were in place?

---

If you do your homework before agreeing to submit a proposal, both you and the client win.

**PUTTING KEY IDEAS INTO ACTION**

- Create a plan for each business development conversation based on whether it is an existing client or prospect, and whether *you* asked for the meeting or *they* asked for the meeting (use the matrix at the beginning of this chapter). Be prepared to change your plan based on how the conversation flows.
- Explore the stakeholders—the influencers—with your client. Ask who will be involved in the decision-making process.
- Never underestimate the importance of gaining emotional commitment to a course of action. Yes, it's important for a client to think, "Sobel has the right experience and methodology to help us achieve our goals." However, that is a necessary but not sufficient factor. They also need to *feel* something like this: "I trust Sobel and am comfortable with him, and if this initiative succeeds,

it's going to make my job easier and help me meet my goals."

- Understanding the "political" dimension of the sale does *not* mean getting involved in organizational politics. Rather, it entails gaining an understanding of the organizational dynamics surrounding a potential contract. Who are the key stakeholders? What kind of exposure or risk will a purchase create for your client? Which influencers will be supportive of the engagement? Which ones will oppose it?
- Use the eight preconditions as a roadmap as you work through the sale and write a proposal. If necessary, be prepared to explain how any given precondition is both important and *in the client's best interest.*

Week

# 6 Free Up a Stuck Sale

I don't understand it," said my exasperated client. "We've done everything right. We have a good relationship with the senior decision-maker. Our solution addresses their need better than anything on the market. But they can't make a decision. It's been dragging on now for months."

Sound familiar? When I ask a large room of my clients, "Are any of you dealing with a sale that's stuck?" almost every hand shoots up.

In this case, the head of strategy for the company was the key decision-maker. She had repeatedly assured my client that it was just a matter of time before they signed the contract. But dates came and went, and there was no sale. I pushed my client to invite her out to lunch and dig deeper. He did, and lo and behold, it turned out that several other senior leaders were holding back their support. In this particular case, the blockage was a lack of *stakeholder alignment*. My client, to his credit, had already inquired about this. But the strategy head had not been forthcoming about the actual situation. It often takes persistence to find out what's really going on.

I suggested he propose an alignment exercise that would involve his client and the other functional and business unit heads. He met individually with each of them, to better understand their needs and concerns and to answer questions about the proposal. Then, using a facilitation template that I helped him design, they had an internal meeting to review the project. This discussion went well, and the sale got unstuck.

## The five preconditions to a sale

When your sale bogs down, there's always a reason. Your job is to find out what that reason is. Most of the time, it's because one of the five preconditions, below, has not been satisfied. Use the illustrative questions I've listed after each precondition to better understand their status.

1. The client must perceive a ***significant problem or opportunity***. You may think there is a problem, but if the client doesn't, there's no sale. I also like to call this the "Red Issue." No red issue, no sale. Of course, plenty of purchases are made for non-urgent staples like pens and paper. My focus, however, is helping you be a rainmaker who addresses important, even mission-critical issues for your clients.
   *Diagnostic questions:*
   - Among your various initiatives, what level of priority does this have?
   - What else in your organization depends on this being fixed?

- How does this relate to your strategy?
- What do you think is the value of fixing this problem/capturing this opportunity?

2. You must be talking to the ***executive who owns the issue***—the person who can take action. If I had a dollar for every hour I have spent with a client executive who was very concerned about a "big" problem, but had no authority to do anything about it, I'd be rich.
   *Diagnostic questions:*
   - In what way does this issue feature into your own performance objectives this year?
   - Will this initiative fall under your bailiwick?
   - Who in your organization will need to authorize a program to address this—is that you, or someone else?
3. There must be a ***healthy dissatisfaction with the rate of change*** or improvement. The client must feel urgency around addressing the need because things aren't happening fast enough or at all. You might have both a significant opportunity and be talking to the right executive. But if the client is not dissatisfied with their current progress—either with their own internal efforts or those of a competitor—there will be no sale.
   *Diagnostic questions:*
   - As you think about this issue, what problems is the status quo causing for you?
   - Can you tell me about previous efforts to address this? (If none, how dissatisfied can they be?)
   - I'm curious, is the challenge that you don't know the right answer or that you're frustrated by the slow speed of improvement?
4. The client must ***trust that you are the highest-value alternative*** to take on the issue. Remember, the biggest competition is often internal. The client must believe you are a better solution than internal efforts or a competitor. Preconditions one to three may be

present, but if the client doesn't think you are the best of all options, there's no sale.

*Diagnostic questions:*

- What options are you thinking about, in terms of using an external resource?
- What are the pros and cons of addressing this internally versus going to the outside for help?
- How do you see our capabilities in this area?

5. The client must believe that the ***key stakeholders are aligned***. Everything can seem in place—i.e., it's an important issue, your client owns it, there is dissatisfaction with the rate of change, and they trust you are the best solution. But the client will still hesitate if the organizational support is not in place in the form of endorsements from key stakeholders.

   *Diagnostic questions:*

   - Who are the key stakeholders? How would you describe their perspectives on this issue?
   - Where does each stakeholder stand, do you think, with regard to whether and how you move forward?
   - Typically, how do you go about getting your internal constituencies aligned for important initiatives like this?

At this point, you may feel I've missed something: A *budget* to buy your solution. If the client has no money—no budget—then there's no sale, right? Wrong. Every client has budget, unless we're talking about a bankrupt entity with no cash in the bank. It is, rather, a question of priorities, as I'll explain below. It's not that the client has no money—they are simply not *prioritizing* their budget for *you.*

## When the preconditions are missing

What if you find one or more of these preconditions is absent? Can you create them? Sometimes you can. In other cases, you may need to walk away and leave the door open for when the conditions are more favorable. Below, I've shared actions you can take if you find a gap.

## Missing Preconditions

1. *No clear, perceived problem or opportunity*
   Actions to consider:
   - Quantify the cost of not acting.
   - Show how much this issue has cost other clients, and the benefits they achieved by tackling it.
   - Get another executive in the organization to convince your client of the urgency of the situation.
   - Find a more urgent issue to discuss.
2. *Executive does not own the issue*
   Actions to consider:
   - Find out who would be the executive sponsor or decision-maker for this issue, and get introduced to them.
   - Have a more senior leader from your organization meet the decision-maker if your contact can't or won't introduce you.
3. *Insufficient dissatisfaction with the rate of improvement*
   Actions to consider:
   - Use client examples to illustrate the speed at which others have solved this problem.
   - Find other stakeholders who are more dissatisfied.
4. *Does not yet trust you are the best, highest-value alternative*
   Actions to consider:
   - Invest to build more credibility and trust in your ability to solve the issue (more face time, more examples, more testimonials, a better benefits case, etc.).
   - Introduce the decision-maker to another client who can describe how you helped them with the same challenge.

5. *Key stakeholders are not aligned*
   Actions to consider:
   - Ask pointed questions about the decision-making process, and who will be involved/who the influencers are.
   - Coach your contact about how you have helped other clients get aligned around issues like this.
   - Offer to prepare collateral for your client that will help with the alignment process.
   - Offer to facilitate discussions/a workshop to achieve greater alignment.

## The four archetypal objections

A client may come up with many different objections to your proposal. Sometimes the answer is clear and straightforward: "We've decided to use someone else." Often, they are vague statements like "We're still reviewing it." All client objections boil down to these four, however:

1. **No Need.** "We don't need what you have to offer."
2. **No Urgency.** "The timing is just not right. We have too many other competing priorities. Maybe in six months we'll be in position to move ahead."
3. **No Trust.** "We like you, but we're not sure your solution is exactly what we're looking for." Or "We like your solution, but we don't feel you're global enough to serve our needs."
4. **No Money.** "We just don't have the budget right now for this."

People used to be taught to "handle" or overcome client objections by convincing the prospect that the objection was not valid. That's a condescending attitude. I see objections as a chance to engage with your clients and understand what they are thinking and the constraints they are up against.

Answer these questions. They will help you get underneath each of these objections.

**No Need.** Is there a different priority or goal you could focus on? Have you made it clear how your solution can help solve an important problem the client has? If the client doesn't recognize they have a need, how could you influence them to see it more clearly?

**No Urgency.** Why is there no urgency? Is it because there are other, more important priorities? Can you help the client see why this *should* be urgent? (Perhaps use an example of another client?) Could you make it easier for the client to get started with you?

To explore the *no urgency* objection, you might ask your client questions such as, "What would change the degree of urgency for you? What other priorities are more important right now? Is your concern that this will take up too much time and energy at a moment when you're very busy, or is it that you don't see solving this problem as being a high priority?"

**No Trust.** What part of the trust equation is weak? Is it that the client doesn't perceive you to be competent—that they don't trust you to deliver? Do they not trust you as much as someone else? Have you had insufficient face time with the client? Do they perceive that your proposal is too risky? You might ask your client directly, "How does your organization perceive us as an option to help address this?"

**No Money.** Is "no money" simply an excuse to cover up one of the other objections that the client doesn't want to admit to? What are the priorities the client is spending money on? When you get this objection, you need to ask some questions to upack what it actually means.

By the way, if "no money" is the stated objection, here are 12 ideas to help you get budget for your proposal:

1. Gain sponsorship from a higher-level, more powerful decision-maker.
2. Redefine the issue so that it is more strategic and can attract the necessary funds.
3. Identify opportunities for the client to create efficiencies in their existing budget.
4. Create flexible contractual terms that reduce the initial financial commitment.
5. Increase the perceived value by improving the benefits case and perceived impact. Tie your work more closely to quantifiable revenue increases or cost reductions.
6. Appeal to an important personal "win" of the buyer.
7. Get additional budget, from other areas that may indirectly benefit from your solution, to fund your proposal.
8. Combine several small discounts—e.g., for volume, scale efficiencies, etc.—to create a large discount.

### THE TRANSFORMATIVE IMPACT OF HAVING MORE LEADS THAN YOU CAN HANDLE OR NEED

The more leads you can generate with current or potential clients, the faster you can grow your business. But there are three other, powerful reasons why it's critical to always have a few more leads than you need or can digest. First, it allows you to turn down the bottom 5 to 10% of opportunities that you see. Over time, this strongly ratchets up the quality of your client portfolio. Second, it enables you to hold much firmer on your pricing, which is no small thing. And third, it puts you in a positive psychological state that helps you approach all your clients as a peer—a valued business partner. The difference between having 15% too many leads and 15% too few leads, in terms of profitability and overall business health, is enormous.

9. Restructure the project to meet the budget they do have (if they have any left!).
10. Rename what you're doing and find a different budget category.
11. Incorporate a small portion of success fees into your contract, so that you are paid in part based on results.
12. If you're outside the client's budget cycle, then work with the client to get your proposal into their next planning and budgeting cycle. You could suggest some modest up-front work to learn more about their needs, build some key relationships ahead of your next proposal iteration, and so on.

Finally, be sure to ask your client how their resource allocation process works. Based on what you learn, what could be done to help your proposal attract interest and attention in their organization?

## Five real client scenarios you will face

Let's look at five real-life examples of possible obstacles or tough questions you will face in winning proposals, either with existing or prospective clients.

### Scenario one: The skeptical client

*You:* "Thanks for meeting with me this morning. I'm looking forward to learning about your challenges and sharing some examples of work we're doing with other companies in your industry."

*Client:* "Great. So tell me about your firm. How would you say you are different?"

For some reason, this question can induce anxiety and sweaty palms in even the most experienced professional. Many people immediately start spouting platitudes like, "We collaborate with our clients" or "We listen well to our clients" or "Our product has superior technology." The problem is that anyone can say these things. In fact, your client has heard them all. They don't really distinguish you.

The difficulty is that it's hard to differentiate yourself through mere descriptions of what you do. What convinces your clients that you are different is engaging them in a value-added conversation about their business issues and offering convincing examples of how you've tackled the issue with other clients.

Here are four sample responses to this question, all of which I have found effective:

*Share what your clients have said.* "When we interview our clients to get their feedback, there are typically three factors they mention. They say that we are . . ." (and then you list three salient points of differentiation). Then you add, "Let me give you an example of one of my recent client engagements where I think we've delivered on those attributes in a very tangible way" (then you describe a brief, 75-to 100-word summary of what happened—the client's problem, your approach, and the results you achieved).

*Focus on people.* "First, let me say that all of the major companies that we compete with have strong technical competence. Where you would really see the differences come out is in the specific team of professionals who work with you day-to-day. I personally focus on a small number of clients, invest significant personal time to get to know them well, and bring them the best our firm has to offer. My starting point is always building an understanding of my client's most important goals and key priorities. Perhaps we could begin there?"

*Go right to client examples.* "The best way to help you understand how we work would be to describe a couple of recent assignments we completed for other clients that have faced a similar challenge." After sharing a couple of brief examples—which you will have picked out in advance because you believe they will resonate with the client—you can then turn the conversation over to the client and ask them about their issues.

*Shift the conversation.* "We're a global firm that helps complex clients optimize their supply chains. I think the best way for me to demonstrate how we are different is by showing you how we would approach a particular logistics issue you are working on. Perhaps you could share the major priorities you're personally focused on this year?"

### Scenario two: The "I want a proposal right now" client

*You* (at the end of the very first conversation): "I enjoyed meeting you and learning more about your efforts to transform your customer experience. Why don't we take a few minutes, before we finish, to talk about next steps."

*Client:* "What would be helpful right now, as a next step, is if you could write a proposal for us, which includes how much this might cost."

As I mentioned in Week 5, you will sometimes be asked to prematurely write a proposal. If the eight preconditions I outlined are not in place, you shouldn't invest your valuable time and money in a proposal effort.

Below, I've set out what I actually said to a potential client in this situation—word for word. She was a feasibility buyer who was demanding a proposal from me after a brief discussion. Remember, a feasibility buyer is someone who can say "no" but not "yes" because he or she is not the ultimate decision-maker.

*Me*: "In order to write a thorough proposal that accurately sets out how we can help you achieve your goals and expected outcomes, there's some more information I need to get."

*Client*: "What kind of information?"

*Me*: "For example, I believe you said your senior vice president of marketing is going to be the executive sponsor of this effort. I'd like to speak with him to understand his perspectives on this challenge and the outcomes he is expecting."

*Client:* "I've already interviewed our SVP and gotten his point of view. That won't be necessary. What I really need is a proposal from you."

*Me:* "That's great, it's good to know you've already done that. I'm curious, what did he say about how this effort will be supported by your IT, human resources, and sales functions? In working with other clients on the customer experience, I've learned that these enterprise-wide linkages are critical to success."

*Client:* "We didn't really explore that. It's a good question, though, that we'll need to answer."

*Me:* "Also, by any chance did you explore the change management dimensions of the initiative? For example, your client service teams are going to have to alter some deep-rooted behaviors. There will probably be shifts in organizational power, as well, which need to be managed. Given the enterprise-wide implications of this challenge, I believe you'll need a project management office, or PMO, with some experienced people assigned to it."

*Client:* "You know, I can't really address those points. Those are things that you'd need to take up with our head of marketing."

*Me:* "Writing a proposal is a big investment for us—and I want to do it right. Without understanding these additional issues, however, it would be hard for me to come up with a plan tailored to your particular situation, or with a firm price. Also, from your SVP's perspective, my experience teaches me that he's going to want to meet up face-to-face with any potential outside resource that you are seriously considering. Perhaps we could conduct this additional discussion with your SVP together?"

*Client:* "Let me discuss it with him, and I'll get back to you."

Sure enough, I got an email two days later inviting me to meet with their SVP of marketing. Notice that, by asking questions, I helped the client realize why it was important for me to get more information before submitting a proposal. I also built my own credibility as someone who was highly experienced in solving the challenge they were facing.

In summary: Gently push back. Don't let yourself get railroaded into writing a proposal that probably has zero chance of achieving liftoff.

### Scenario three: Competing against an incumbent

Clients ask for proposals even when an existing supplier is already meeting their needs. Sometimes they do it just to put pressure on the incumbent. Sometimes there is a dissatisfaction of some kind, and they want to see what someone else could do. Often, internal regulations require multiple bids for large contracts, no matter how good a job the incumbent is doing. But beware: I've seen data from my own clients on this, and the success rate when there is an incumbent is low. So you need to think such opportunities through very carefully, and have an incisive strategy if you decide to proceed.

Here are nine suggestions that can help you gain some wallet share from or even unseat an incumbent competitor:

1. *Look for trigger events.* I also call these "buying catalysts." There are certain circumstances that will make it easier to break in, such as:
   - A dissident shareholder or threat of takeover
   - Executive changes, such as a new CEO, or a corporate reorganization
   - Economic events or shocks
   - A notable change in company strategy
   - Turnover or retirements at the competition
   - A service or quality failure on the part of the incumbent
   - New competitive threats that have developed
2. *Try to identify something small or non-threatening that you can work on.* If a client has a good relationship with an existing provider, and needs to dump that provider in order to hire you, your chances of success are limited.
3. *Be a contrarian.* Propose a new way of defining the problem. Show how their current approach is outmoded ("We used to do it that way . . .").
4. *Focus on an area where you are clearly differentiated or have a tangible strength vis-à-vis your competitor.* Ask yourself, "Where do we have a special competency we can leverage?"
5. *Invest to earn the client's trust and respect.* The incumbent has the advantage of an existing relationship of trust. You're going to have to go the extra mile and make an up-front investment in understanding the client's issues and organization.

6. *Identify executives in the client organization who are not as loyal to the incumbent.* It will be easier to capture the attention and interest of these individuals. You may be able to divide and conquer, as they say!
7. *Emphasize innovation and new ideas.* Clients are always looking for fresh perspectives, and they will usually not let an existing relationship get in the way of at least listening to someone else's insights. Develop an intriguing point of view about one of their critical issues, and you'll most likely get a hearing.
8. *Be patient and persistent.* It may take many visits and numerous conversations, over a prolonged period—months or even a year or two—to find the right opening.
9. *Stay in touch so you are on their radar when an opportunity comes up.* This applies to any new business development situation, but even more so when there is a major, established competitor. When an urgent issue arises, you want to be top of mind.

If you are being blocked by an incumbent competitor, which of these nine strategies would be particularly helpful? What special strength could you bring to the table?

### Scenario four: Moving up when your client is jealous and controlling

A company I advised had a major contract with a large corporation. Their day-to-day client was a director-level executive who was insecure about his position. My client felt they had a compelling idea, with enterprise-wide implications, for improving that company's business. So they decided to bring it to the attention of the senior vice president, who was two levels above their director contact. They told the director, in passing, that they were going to see the SVP. At the time, he just nodded and didn't seem at all troubled. But the move created a firestorm. The director complained bitterly to the SVP, which then raised serious doubts in the SVP's mind about the wisdom of holding a meeting without his director present, or even having one at all. The director also angrily confronted my client for going around him. In a flash, they lost the reservoir of trust they had built up.

If your day-to-day contact in your client's organization is a mid-level executive, you're going to be drawn to establish relationships in senior management. But sometimes executives are controlling and even jealous of your loyalties. They want to be your singular client, period. And they certainly don't want you going over their heads.

So how do you "move up" in the organization and still bring your existing client along with you? Here are four things you should do:

1. Focus above all on building trust with your day-to-day clients. When they say, "I don't want you to talk to my boss," they are betraying a mistrust of your intentions. Invest in one-on-one time to really understand their aspirations and fears—what makes them tick. Show them you are unequivocally dedicated to helping them achieve their goals. Articulate why it will be helpful to *them* for you to have a relationship with their boss.
2. During the sales process you should do your best to meet with the senior stakeholders and executives whose areas will be impacted by the delivery of your product or service. This way, you will already have a pre-established relationship with these executives.
3. When you are in the delivery phase, continue to create opportunities to meet with senior management as part of your startup process. With your immediate client, discuss the need to gain these leadership perspectives and help ensure management's support and commitment going forward.
4. Once you have an ongoing relationship, get exposure for your work in the wider organization. Find

opportunities to interact with the key stakeholders in order to maintain their support for your engagement. Connect what you're doing to the organization's broader strategy. Look for opportunities, such as in planning sessions and internal conferences, to present the results you're achieving.

## Scenario five: Dealing with "ghosting"

Have you ever had a highly engaging conversation with a potential client, who seemed quite enthusiastic and interested in what you had to offer—but then . . . nothing happened? You may have met several times, or even written a proposal. But the client just never got back to you.

I know several companies, in fact, who have determined that "no decision" is one of the most prevalent reasons for registering a proposal "loss"—they simply never hear back from the client. Each of them has hundreds of millions of dollars in proposals outstanding with clients who have just never made a decision.

You're not alone. It seems that over the last decade there has been a dramatic increase in what I can only describe as rude and unprofessional behavior in the business world. Maybe it's due to the overload that many corporate managers now feel in an always-on, 24/7 workplace culture. Or perhaps it's part of a broader cultural trend, where self-absorption has pushed aside civility. Thus my use of the term "ghosting," which comes from the dating world. It's when someone stops answering your texts, emails, calls, and other communications with no explanation. The person turns into a ghost, for all practical purposes.

First, don't get emotional about it. It's just business. Feeling like a failure, or worrying about it in the middle of the night, won't change anything. Usually, the lack of a response has little to do with you and the value of what you're offering, and everything to do with issues the client is grappling with. Clients lose interest for many reasons. Haven't you ever started shopping for a big-ticket purchase, only to change your mind after a week of surfing the Internet? Sometimes other priorities intrude. Sometimes a client is, literally, just shopping around to see what's out there.

Second, make sure you stick to your client development process. Just because another driver on the road is running a red light doesn't mean you should, too. In other words, don't suddenly send a client an email with an unsolicited proposal, or abruptly tell them you'll give them a discount in a bid to recapture their interest.

Third, give yourself three more tries at re-establishing contact. These could be emails, phone messages, text messages, calls to their EA, handwritten notes, and so on. If you strike out, then take a break from pursuing the opportunity. More than three tries and you'll start to sound desperate. And besides, if they don't respond after three attempts, they probably aren't going to respond after four or five!

For your last communication you should write an email or note that goes something like this:

> Dear Susan,
> I hope you are doing well. I wanted to make sure you had seen my last email, which contained a link to a recent article I wrote on how leadership can support the development of a "clients for life" culture.
>
> At this point, I'm assuming the initiative we discussed is no longer a high priority for you, or else you don't feel it's productive to continue our conversations about it. In any event, I would be delighted to re-engage with you again on this issue at a future date.
>
> All the best,
> Andrew

Then, move on.

**PUTTING KEY IDEAS INTO ACTION**

- Think about a sale or business development conversation you are involved with right now, with either an existing or prospective client. Review each of the five preconditions to buy and rate them as A, B, or C. A = Fully Present, B = Somewhat Present, and C = Absent. What steps can you take to solidify the preconditions that you rated B or C?
- Is there a client with whom you're sensing any of the four fundamental objections? (No Need, No Urgency, No Trust, No Money). Formulate one or two questions you'd like to ask them to help explore what's behind the objection.
- Identify a current or prospective client that is experiencing a trigger event—for example, a reorganization, competitive threat, new CEO, change in strategy, etc. How can your solutions address the need created by that "buying catalyst"?

# Week 7 Anticipate and Agenda Set

Have you ever been in a meeting with a client who seemed distracted? Perhaps you noticed her eyes wandering, or saw him reach for his smartphone. Or have you tried to get an appointment with an executive who just wouldn't make room in the schedule for you?

In both cases, the problem is the same. You're not compelling enough. You're not showing how *you* are relevant to the client's agenda of critical priorities.

How would you react if your plumber called you and suggested you get together for lunch so you could get to know each other better? How about if you got a call from your doctor, who asked you to come in to discuss your latest test results? Who would you make time for?

Clients are like the rest of us—they open their schedules for their most essential priorities.

If you want to be seen as integral to your clients' growth and profitability, you have to demonstrate that what you do is strategic to their business. You must show that you are proactively focused on their most important goals. You need to demonstrate you can help them see around the corner and anticipate important, future influences on their business.

## Do you really understand your client's agenda?

Every client has an agenda of three to five priorities or goals that they are focused on in their organization. It's rarely more than five, because after four or five they tail off in importance. And usually it's not fewer than three.

Client executives also typically have a set of three to five *personal* priorities. These are important to understand because if you aspire to build a trusted relationship with clients, you need to appreciate their total context. And there may very well be some personal interests or needs that you can help them with. One of my clients, for example, was interested in getting on a corporate board. I gave advice on this, and introduced the person to several top executive search firms that have specialty boardroom practices.

A professional priority might be to implement a new project management system, or to reduce costs. For senior business heads, it could be to expand into a new market, or make several strategic hires to augment their top team. Personal agenda items could include getting promoted, building a network, or helping their family adjust to living in a new city. It completely depends on the person and where he or she is in the organization.

I often am asked, "We are in a very competitive marketplace. How can we more effectively differentiate ourselves?" One of the best ways to do that is to learn more about your clients' priorities, needs, and goals than any other competitor knows.

I had a client who was the top performing partner in his firm. Every year he consistently generated tens of millions of dollars in new revenue—mostly from his existing clients. One day I took him out to lunch and asked him about the secret to his success. He pulled a small square of wrinkled paper out of his suit pocket. "Andrew, do you see this sheet of paper? On it, I've printed the names of all my key executive clients. And next to each name I've noted their one or two most important goals for this year. *My* job is to help them successfully accomplish those goals." He didn't define himself as a consultant who did strategy work or was an expert in re-engineering. Rather, his core mission was simply to help his clients accomplish their most important priorities.

## How well do you know your clients?

By now, you may be thinking, "I know my clients pretty well. I'm doing ok at this agenda-setting thing." But let me push back. I frequently ask large groups of very senior relationship managers and account executives—partners, managing directors, VPs, etc.—how well they understand their clients' agendas. Here's the question: "For what percentage of your clients would you say you have a thorough understanding of their three to five most critical professional priorities? How about their personal agendas?"

For their largest clients—their key accounts—the answers are usually 50% (e.g., for half their clients they have a thorough understanding of the professional agenda) and 20% (personal agenda). On average, for *all* their clients, people usually say 20% and 10%. I call that flying blind. If you don't know your client's agenda, you are like an airplane pilot with no radar and no map.

What would these figures be for you and your clients?

The takeaway here is that many client-facing professionals actually have a poor understanding of their clients' agenda. They may know what that agenda is in their specific sphere of expertise, but not the broader set of priorities I'm referring to here.

## Three stages to agenda setting

There are three stages to becoming an agenda-setter. First, you *react.* A client calls you up and says, "We need help with this problem." That's great when it happens, but if that's how you get all your business—waiting for the phone to ring—you're a reactive, expert-for-hire. Besides, by the time the client decides what they want to do, they may very well be talking to several of your competitors as well.

Second, you *sense.* Using various techniques, which I'll discuss shortly, you uncover the client's agenda. This is not as easy as it sounds. After all, are *you* willing to fully reveal yourself to someone you don't know very well or perhaps even just met?

It's often difficult to discern what your client's true agenda is. This is especially true as you go higher up in the organization. One of my clients, for example, a division CEO, had a four-part strategy he was very visibly following. But he had another very important agenda as well that involved building up his top team of direct reports. That wasn't in the annual report or his strategic plan. But after several in-depth conversations, this priority came to light. When I demonstrated I had experience and ideas that would help him in this area, he ultimately asked me to work with his executives and coach them.

Third, you *anticipate.* This is what separates the advisor from the expert-for-hire. As one executive told me, "My trusted advisor is always thinking two or three moves ahead. She is bringing me ideas and insights about trends, best practices, and competitive changes that may affect our business six, 12, or 18 months from now." By anticipating, you become an agenda-setter. You understand, inform, and ultimately shape and influence your client's agenda.

This is a subtle process. It's rare that someone can walk into an organization from the outside and wow the leadership by revealing something of great importance that no one has thought of before. More likely, you slowly shape your client's perspectives.

One of my clients, for example, severely lagged in implementing industry specialization in their sales organization. Since their competitors were not very far along, either, they felt no need to change their plans. But their own industry was slow-moving and hardly a showcase for leading-edge management practices. Over a number of sessions I showed them how many leading companies in other markets were using an industry focus to drive substantial revenue growth. As a result, they dramatically accelerated efforts to organize around the key industries they served.

Anticipatory agenda setting can also be about implementation. A mid-sized client once retained me to help them implement a key account management program. We agreed on the goal, but I disagreed with many of my client's views on how to go about achieving it. For example, overnight, they wanted to designate several hundred clients as key accounts. I shared with them how some other clients of mine had done this, and the risks of starting with so many clients. Over the course of several discussions, I got them to agree to start with a pilot of just 20 accounts, to test and prove the concept.

I also helped them anticipate several problems they had not thought of. I warned them that relationship managers whose clients were not included in the program were going to feel excluded and even resentful. I then suggested several ways to mitigate this reaction. They also wanted to start with a 35-page account planning template. I told them that the emphasis had to be on creative, dynamic planning discussions, and that a shorter, five-page plan was not only sufficient but would get greater uptake from their people.

## The key to sole-source business

Agenda setting is simple in concept but hard to execute well. First, you have to be a real student of both the external factors that may affect your client's business as well as internal organizational dynamics.

Second, you must penetrate more deeply into your client's forward planning cycle. Figure 7.1 illustrates this.

If you wait to get calls from your client about a need they have already identified, you'll find yourself in the lower-right corner, where you are "agenda reacting." Here, procurement—pictured as a hungry alligator—will

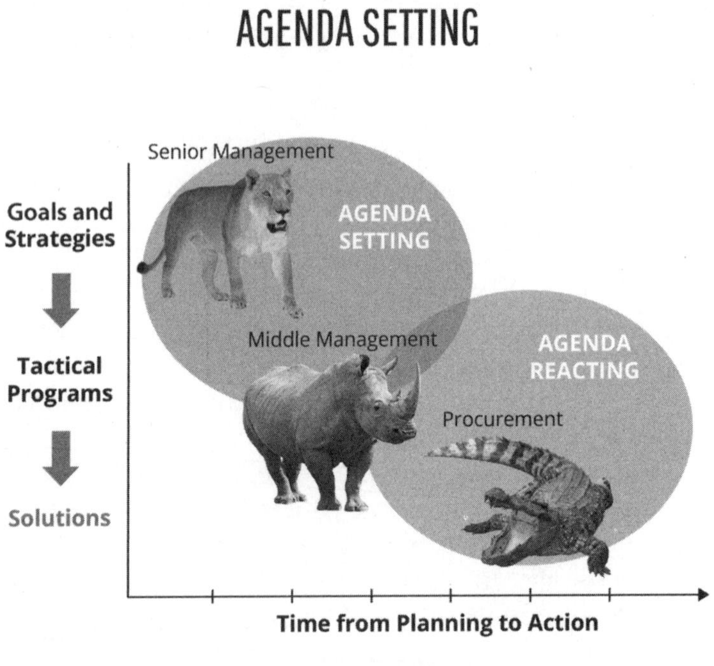


**Figure 7.1** Agenda setting

be biting at your ankles. The client may very well be requesting proposals from multiple suppliers. There will also be much less opportunity to reframe the issue. At this point, the problem definition will be well established in the client's mind, and you'll have to take it or leave it.

Where I want you to be is in the upper-left corner. Here, you are discussing your client's future plans and priorities. You are bringing them value-added thought leadership in the form of insightful points of view, best practices, trends, and so on. By working together with the client to define the need, you'll have an excellent chance to win sole-source business.

## Don't be a walking cliché

A senior executive I recently interviewed gave me an earful about how *not* to learn about her agenda. She told me: "I'm tired of hearing, 'What keeps you up at night?'—which is just a lazy question. Another one is 'What does success look like?' Salespeople have been asking these for 30 years. I also get the 'What are your top three priorities?' approach. They take notes, and then say, 'We can help you with number two.'"

You should come across as a potential business advisor who has a lot of wisdom to share, not a salesperson looking for a quick sale.

I find five different techniques very effective in sensing your client's agenda. First, despite my admonition in Week 3 not to *over-prepare*, you do need to *prepare*. As one executive told me, "You need to show up knowing the outlines of our strategy and what's important to us as an organization." Remember—you just need a couple of hooks to engage your client. One of my clients was a master at this. He was an expert in executive compensation. He often found the clues to formulate penetrating questions in his prospective client's 10K report. He would tell a client something like, "I noticed that your treatment of deferred compensation is a little unusual." Then he would go on to explain how most of his other clients did it, adding, "I'm curious, how did you make that decision?"

### LOWER THE THRESHOLD FOR A CLIENT MEETING

A well-known banker once said to me, "If I waited until I had a great idea to go see a client, I would only leave my office once a year." His point was that you don't need a brilliant new idea or a finely tuned PowerPoint presentation to go and have a cup of coffee with a client and talk about how he or she is doing. Don't make it difficult to go see clients and prospects. Lower your threshold to have a brief meeting. The more clients you talk to, the more opportunities you'll have to uncover an important issue that someone is struggling with. And the more you'll learn about what's happening in your market.

The second approach, which you have to be cautious with, is direct questioning—e.g., "What are your top priorities for the business this year?" My experience is that the higher up you go, the less effective this question is. A top executive may not want to open up to you right away, and she may also expect you to already have a reasonable idea of what's going on in the company. Try this, but be aware it may not be the most fresh and engaging strategy. Sometimes, I make this more personal and ask, "Of the various initiatives you have going, which are you *personally* going to be highly involved with?"

A third approach is to ask *implication questions*. For example, I recently met with a prospective client whose new strategy was quite public. I was having a conversation with the chief learning officer (CLO). My opening questions were, "I'm familiar with your new strategy aimed at repositioning your firm in the large corporate segment. How is this impacting your priorities in learning and development? What new capabilities and skills do your people need to develop to facilitate this shift?" Similarly, you could ask implication questions about external trends or competitive changes. By posing these well-formulated but indirect questions, you establish your own credibility and begin to draw out the client's agenda.

A fourth strategy is to ask what I call emotional or personal questions, which I'll cover in more detail in Week 10. These questions get at your clients' dreams and aspirations, as well as their fears and anxieties. The question, "As you look out two or three years, what are your aspirations for this business?" is more interesting than the dry and clichéd "What are your top three priorities?"

A final approach is to simply ask, "I'm curious, at the end of the year, how will your own performance be evaluated? What are the key objectives you've been asked to meet?" If necessary, I add, "I ask all my clients this question. I find that the more I know about my clients' goals, the more helpful I can be."

## How agenda setting works

A client of mine wanted to build a relationship with a large retail bank. Through a contact who had worked at the bank, my client got an introduction to the head of the private banking division. They believed the bank was missing a major opportunity to cultivate younger professionals as clients. So they did a survey of their *own* Millennial employees, who matched this demographic, to better understand their attitudes toward savings and money management. When they met with the CEO of the private bank, they shared the results of their research, accompanied by some tentative recommendations about how the CEO could set about capturing this growing market segment. The CEO was blown away by my client's preparation and insights. They procured a major, sole-source engagement to help develop and implement a new "young professionals" strategy for the bank.

While this type of agenda setting may seem outside your reach, it does illustrate the power of anticipating your clients' needs. There are many smaller but nonetheless impactful things you can do to agenda set with your clients.

## Four agenda-setting strategies

The very first thing I recommend is to schedule a regular agenda-setting conversation with all of your established clients. Position it like this: "With our best clients, we meet periodically to step back from our day-to-day work together and talk about the big picture surrounding the engagement. It's a chance for us to share our latest thinking, talk about best practices from other client engagements we're involved with, and give you our observations about improvement opportunities within your organization. It's also a chance for you to share with us your evolving plans and priorities and any corporate initiatives that may impact our work."

A second agenda-setting strategy is to regularly share points of view about your clients' business, their challenges, key trends, and so on. This could be as simple as talking about how some of your other clients are tackling the same issues.

A third and very effective strategy is what I call the "deep dive." Offer to facilitate a working session on an important issue your client is facing. This could be over lunch, or even a half-day workshop. If you work with a large firm, bring other expert colleagues along. One top executive I interviewed referred to this as "the ticket to entry" for a major provider they worked with. He explained: "One year, we were very focused on asset utilization across the company. This firm put on a one-day workshop on strategies to increase asset productivity. They brought a bunch of their experts, and we fielded a team of our people who were involved in various internal initiatives in this area." The result? The firm rapidly became this company's provider of choice in their area of expertise.

Finally, if you work with a large firm, systematically gather intel from other colleagues and team members who are working on the client account. What are they seeing and hearing? During a panel discussion that I moderated, a client executive highlighted the value of this: "You are a major supplier to my company," he told the audience. "You know as much or more about our operations than most of the outside providers we work with. Tell me what you're learning. Give me ideas about how to improve our business."

## Ignore the barriers

Many factors will conspire to keep you from agenda setting with clients. Don't let them! You'll find that most of your client conversations are about operational execution and product and service delivery, and it's hard to carve out the time to take the big-picture view that agenda setting demands. In some cases you'll feel that your client is too junior to practice agenda setting with. Other times, you'll get cold feet because you think you won't be able to carry on that higher-level discussion about the client's business. Most of these barriers are manageable. Break through them—you owe it to your client to excel at anticipatory agenda setting.

**PUTTING KEY IDEAS INTO ACTION**

- Select your three most important clients. How well do you understand the professional and personal agendas of your key contacts? What can you do to fill in your knowledge gaps?
- Think about an upcoming client meeting. How could you turn it into more of an agenda-setting conversation? Specifically:
  - How can you engender a deeper discussion about your client's future plans and priorities than would be typical for an operational update?

(*continued*)

**PUTTING KEY IDEAS INTO ACTION (*CONT'D*)**

- What new ideas or perspectives can you introduce in the meeting?
- What questions can you ask to learn more about your client's agenda?
- How can you more directly tie your work to the client's most important strategic or operational goals?

**ADDITIONAL FREE RESOURCES FOR YOU**

Download my free *Client Growth Guide* at www.andrewsobel.com/growth-guide. It includes two worksheets to help you with Agenda Setting: How Well Do You Really Know Your Client and How Well Do You Really Know Your Client's Organization.

# Week 8 Reframe for Maximum Impact

A technology company asked me to help transform their customer service managers (CSMs) into proactive, trusted advisors to their corporate clients. As a small first step, we started with a one-day workshop for their CSMs on the skills of the trusted advisor. By the end of the day, however, I knew the effort was misguided. I needed to reframe both the problem and the solution.

It turned out their software had some significant glitches. Their sales team would go in and sell the promise of dramatic business improvements, but once the system was installed, the complaints started. Many customers, who had signed multi-year contracts, became resentful and angry. I also learned that the CSMs had vastly different levels of skills and experience, and required very different types of training. Furthermore, their customers had quite different needs. Their smallest accounts, in fact, didn't need a highly skilled "trusted advisor" at all—just someone they could call once in a while with questions.

Truth be told, I had probed most of these issues during my initial meeting with the client's CEO, but he had brushed them aside. She stuck to her vision of an army of trusted advisors serving every customer.

In my subsequent conversation with the CEO, I told her that we needed to restate the goal of the initiative. The focus should not be for every CSM to be a trusted advisor to all their accounts. Rather, it was to build long-term customer loyalty through service and support that was tailored to each client's needs and expectations. I then suggested that an enterprise-wide view of his challenge dictated a new sequence of actions: First, the software problems absolutely had to be fixed. Then and only then could CSMs be re-skilled. Otherwise, there would be frustration and cynicism. I also recommended creating three tiers of CSMs, certified to serve three distinct client segments—small clients, medium-size clients, and large key accounts. The CSMs were completely on board with this approach.

By reframing the problem in an enterprise-wide context, and challenging my client's assumptions, the initiative was transformed. It evolved from a narrow training program into a holistic strategy for a new, comprehensive approach to client development and management.

## Defining the totality of the Issue

Reframing is the art and science of defining the right problem, the total problem, and the total solution. The great physicist Albert Einstein alluded to the importance of this when he wrote, "If I had only one hour to save the world, I would spend fifty-five minutes defining the problem, and only five minutes finding the solution."

Reframing is a powerful but rare skill. The good news is that it can be practiced and learned.

For many different reasons, executives will often narrowly define their issue. It could be that the client works in a functional silo (e.g., HR, IT, finance, etc.) and simply doesn't have an enterprise-wide view. Sometimes, clients lack experience in solving the issue. They may confuse symptoms for the root cause and/or underestimate what it will really take to fix it.

Reframing can be threatening to a client. When an executive realizes that the relatively straightforward task of putting in a new IT system is not going to actually fix the problem without concomitantly improving people's skills and behaviors, redesigning work flows, and making other major changes, it can be jarring.

So you will often meet resistance when you try to reframe. Think about this: How would you feel if you decided to add another bathroom to your house, but were told by the contractor that you also needed to upgrade your entire plumbing system in order for the new bathroom to work properly? You may see the validity of your contractor's proposal, but you probably won't be happy about spending twice as much as you had planned.

## Three reframing principles

Here are three principles to help clients become comfortable with your reframing.

First, *the client must feel ownership of the new frame.* You can't force it on them. You have to work with your client and get them to embrace the new frame. This means patiently collaborating with them to flesh out the new problem definition and scope of the solution.

Second, *your client must feel an emotional connection to the new frame.* An intellectual understanding is not enough. The old adage—"facts tell and emotions sell"—is still valid. If clients are confronted with the need to expand or alter the scope of an initiative, they won't truly buy into it unless there is both a rational and emotional commitment. Make appeals to their right brain—to their dreams, aspirations, desire for legacy, and so on. Show how it will help them personally succeed. Illustrate why your approach reduces their risk.

The third principle is that *you must put your client in the new frame.* The new frame, for example, might change the balance of power in the organization. You must show the executive you're working with how this can further their goals and interests. They need to see how and where they fit into the new order.

Next, I'll explore two types of reframing with you. I call them *incremental reframing* and *radical reframing.*

## Using the compass method for incremental reframing

Incremental reframing is when you expand the client's understanding of the problem in small steps rather than dramatic leaps.

For example, a client of mine had a recurring product quality problem. They had tried again and again to improve the manufacturing processes, but could not get to the consistency of quality they wanted. A consultant I recommended was able to identify both upstream design issues and downstream customer use problems that

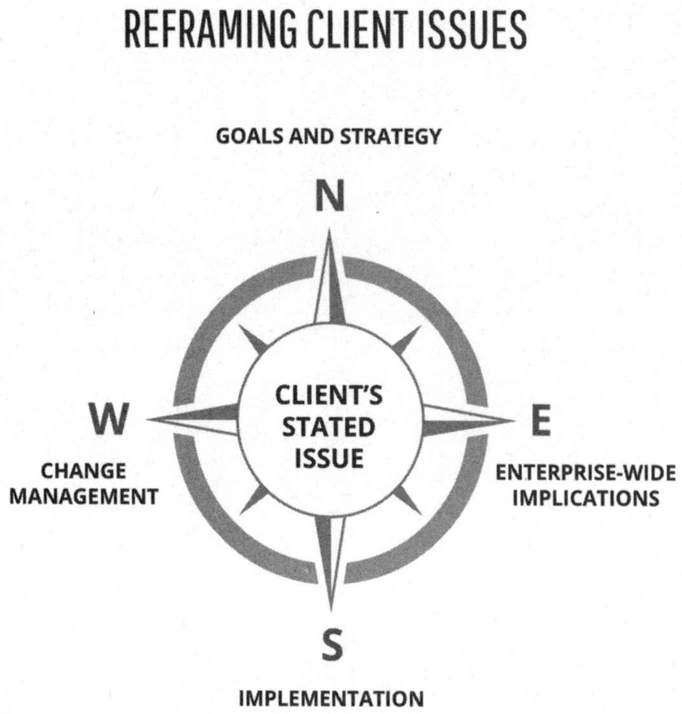


**Figure 8.1** Reframing client issues

needed to be fixed. He helped the client broaden their definition of the problem by shining a light on adjacent functions that were contributing to poor product quality.

There are four main directions you can explore to create incremental reframing, shown in Figure 8.1. Let's look at them one by one. Think of this, metaphorically, as a compass with four directions: north, south, east, and west.

### North: Reframing into strategy

When you reframe upstream into strategy, you put the desired solution or transaction in the context of the company's overarching goals and strategy. By doing so, it becomes more important and mission-critical. You can ask questions like:

- Which key strategic priorities does this support right now?
- If you wanted this initiative to be seen as clearly aligning with your most important, enterprise-wide strategies, is there anything you'd change or do differently?
- Can you tell me more about the overall context for this program? Why have you decided to pursue it now?

When you reframe into strategy it doesn't mean you'll necessarily be working on the strategy. Rather, by clearly connecting your solution to the organization's higher-level goals, the issue will be seen as more strategic than it might have been. This makes it easier for the client to get comfortable with a new perspective, and more willing to invest in addressing the issue.

### South: Reframing into implementation

In 1962, Ross Perot was a young salesperson with IBM. He believed that IBM's clients needed more help to deploy and manage the mainframe computers that IBM sold them. When Perot suggested to his boss that there was a potential business in assisting clients to better utilize IBM's hardware, he was told to forget about it and stick to selling computers. So he quit IBM and founded Electronic Data Systems (EDS). It became a multi-billion-dollar company that pioneered computer facilities management and IT outsourcing. Perot became a billionaire when EDS was sold to General Motors for $2.5 billion. HP later purchased the company for a whopping $13.9 billion in 2008.

Executives need to rapidly turn a proposed solution into value for their business. Framing your product or service in an implementation context can therefore be extremely valuable—in Perot's case, he started an entire company based on this idea. You can explore implementation considerations with questions like these:

- What are the challenges in implementing this?
- In the past, what have you done to ensure a solution like this is used and implemented properly?
- From your perspective, what are the implementation risks? How can they be mitigated?

### East: Reframing across the enterprise

The first two reframing vectors are upstream into strategy and downstream into implementation. I call the third direction *reframing across the enterprise.*

There are vast interdependencies in any complex organization, but middle managers are often in silos where their points of view are local and their compensation rewards them for success in their own bailiwick. Any improvement initiative will typically have a knock-on effect that ripples across other functions and business units.

One of my clients, for example, implemented a new customer relationship management (CRM) system at great cost. But to work effectively, there needed to be collaboration from many other parts of the organization to gather and update the data. The new CRM had to mesh seamlessly with other systems, and there were cultural inhibitions about sharing information that had to be overcome. It took them another year to get the CRM to work properly because they had not thought of it as an enterprise-wide issue, just a sales and IT issue. The healthcare industry faces similar challenges as doctors migrate from taking notes with pen and pencil to maintaining highly detailed, cloud-based medical records.

To surface these enterprise-wide interdependencies, you have to ask a lot of questions about how your solution or product will interact with other functions and business units. You might start with simply, "What other parts of your organization will be impacted by this?" or "What are some of the challenges you face in leveraging this across your business?"

## West: Reframing around change management

The first three strategies for expansive reframing take us up, down, and across the organization. The fourth strategy says you need to take a process or change management perspective around any major new intervention or solution. This is an additional area to explore with your client that will inform and possibly enlarge the scope of what you do.

There are (at least) five major dimensions that should be considered:

1. *Stakeholder alignment and management.* Who are the key stakeholders from within the area you're working, but also from other parts of the company? How should this group be communicated to and managed? How can you ensure their ongoing support?
2. *Technology and systems.* This is a hugely important and complex area—many corporations invest over $1 billion a year just on information technology. You may know little about this area, but it behooves you to ask some basic questions and ensure your client's systems will support, not obstruct, your solution.
3. *Management process.* Management process comprises the decision-making protocols, supporting systems, and roles and responsibilities that surround the area you are working in. For starters, you need to understand who is going to be responsible for implementation. How will they monitor and assess progress? Let's say you have a solution that helps companies capture new data about their customers buying habits. Who

gets access to this information? How is it incorporated into decision making about customer management and new product development? How does this impact managers' roles and responsibilities?

4. *People and skills.* This is one of the primary concerns of leaders, but not always of middle management, who are more focused on their individual contribution versus building talent across the organization. You should ask: What are the implications of our work for the people and skills you will need, both today and in the future?
5. *Organization structure.* This represents your client's organizational hard wiring. You might ask: How well do you feel your current organization structure supports an initiative like this? What changes to your organization might you consider in the future in order to maximize the return from this investment? On the other side of the coin, many companies think that reorganizing will fix a multitude of ills. I've had some clients who change their organization structure about every 18 months in an endless quest to solve issues that need other types of solutions to fix.

In short, whenever a client presents an issue to you, you should carefully explore all four directions of the compass:

- How can this initiative best align with and support the strategy?
- Have the implementation implications been thoroughly explored and planned for?
- What are the cross-enterprise implications of your work?
- What change management dimensions need to be guided and directed in order to ensure success?

## Radical reframing strategies

The compass approach is designed to identify incremental or gradual changes to the scope of your engagement. They will help you expand and broaden the canvas you're painting on with the client.

There are also what I call *radical reframing* options. You will probably use these less often than the compass method, but they can be extremely powerful.

There are five principle techniques that will help you create a potentially radical reframing.

### Highlight opposites

When I was a country CEO for Gemini Consulting, one of our top business developers for Europe met with a senior executive at a major telecommunications company. This was during the early 1990s when "reengineering" was all the rage. The executive was polite, but told him firmly, "We are all set with our reengineering program, and we're going to work with one of your competitors to implement it."

My colleague became quiet. He looked at the window, and then back at the client. He said, softly, "We *used* to do reengineering."

The client was stunned, and even a bit angry. "What do you mean? 'Used to?' What are you saying?"

Suddenly, the executive was fully engaged in the conversation. My colleague explained that we had developed a new approach that integrated changes in technology, business processes, and people skills to capture far more benefits than reengineering alone. In an instant, his perceptions changed. Their ready-to-launch reengineering program suddenly looked old and tired before it even got off the ground. The result? Three months later my firm won a $30 million project spanning several years.

My colleague had reframed "New" as "Old." He reframed by highlighting the opposite. You can use this approach, too, by saying "We *used* to do it that way."

Other illustrative examples of highlighting opposites could include:

- Telling a client who wants to lower prices that he should actually be raising them
- Telling a client who wants to hire you for a project that they should actually do it themselves—but that they should consider hiring you for something entirely different
- Suggesting to a client who wants to grow a business that she should actually be shrinking or divesting it

### Reprioritize

Sometimes, your client wants to do something that is a misplaced priority. Your job is to convince them to reorder their priorities and shift their focus. How do you do this? I always take clients back to their fundamental objectives. What are they trying to accomplish? What's the fastest way to get there? What actions need to be prioritized, given those objectives?

For example, I had a client whose profit margins had steadily declined due to a lack of innovation and increased global competition. They wanted to embark on a culture change initiative to help restore their financial health. This was going to be a nine-month effort led by an outside firm that specialized in this area. I asked them to list all the factors that had contributed to their eroding profitability. They included poor financial controls, outdated operational processes, and stale products. I pointed out that their singular priority should be to fix the "hard" systems that would immediately increase personal accountability for results. This, I insisted, would in turn stimulate a cultural change. They had prioritized the wrong starting point.

### HOW INSISTENT SHOULD YOU BE ABOUT REFRAMING A CLIENT'S ISSUES?

Country music star Kenny Rogers, in his number one hit "The Gambler," sings, "You've got to know when to hold 'em, know when to fold 'em." So, how adamant should you be? Sometimes, a client will just say to you, "You're making some good points, but this is what we want to do right now." The best outcome is when, through your careful explorations of the issue, the client begins to realize that the scope needs to be larger. If that doesn't happen, it can be helpful to share an example from another client that illustrates the value and importance of a broader perspective. In the end, you have to be willing to accept the client's starting point, unless to do so will seriously jeopardize their success and your reputation.

## Challenge assumptions

There is always a set of assumptions that underpin a client request, and sometimes, they are wrong. Years ago I worked on a team that was consulting to the government of a South American country. The work was sponsored by the World Bank. My team was assigned to review the copper mining industry in the country (rather far afield from what I do today, but that was the task). The plans all looked great. The companies involved in copper mining and smelting were losing tons of money, but were all projected to become highly profitable in just a few years. They wanted us to help them put together a growth plan that included acquiring more mines and expanding their infrastructure.

Not surprisingly, everything in their plans depended on one big assumption: The price of copper. Our team questioned their price forecasts, but we did not challenge them very strongly. The consultant in charge of the overall project for my firm, however—a brilliant Spaniard who was also a business school professor—would have none of it. I had to sit through a seven-hour marathon review meeting that he presided over, held in a small, sweltering conference room. He ripped our work apart and demonstrated that the underlying pricing forecast was unrealistic. I remember leaving the room with my shirt literally soaked in sweat from the stress of the professor's onslaught. He was right, though.

The companies wanted to expand. But the right project was actually to restructure the entire sector and dramatically reduce costs in the face of copper prices that were more likely to go down than up over the next three years.

You have to ask your client: What are the key assumptions underlying your plans? And then, you have to diplomatically engage them in a discussion about their assumptions, challenging them where merited. The result may be that you define a very different solution than what was initially proposed.

### Identify the root cause

Sakichi Toyoda was the founder of the Toyoda industrial conglomerate in Japan, which later included the Toyota car manufacturing business. He told his engineers that if they asked "Why" five times, they would discover the root cause of any quality problem—and also, usually, the solution. ("Why are there scratches on the door paint? Because the painting equipment isn't working properly. Why is that happening? There is a software error. Why is there a software error? And so on . . .). Getting to the root cause of a client's problem is therefore a very good way to reframe what is required.

The propensity of large corporations to repeatedly reorganize is a symptom of poor root cause analysis. I had a client who wanted to completely restructure his company's organization chart. The CEO told me the organization had become dysfunctional and was making decisions too slowly. After conducting some interviews, I realized that there was really nothing wrong with the existing structure. The problem was the chief operating officer. He had been promoted beyond his level of competency and had become a bottleneck for virtually every important decision. He was a weak leader who didn't know how to delegate. I told my client that the COO ought to be moved aside. He agreed. As it turned out, that single step unfroze the organization and obviated the need to redesign the whole organization. The root cause was not an outdated organization structure—it was a weak leader who was gumming up the works.

### Expose the inconsistency of their beliefs

One of the best ways to change someone's point of view is to expose the inconsistency of his or her beliefs. For example, I was asked to do some work for a company whose mission and values talked at length about always acting in a "customer-centric" way and "putting customers first." They also highlighted the importance of realizing "the full potential of each employee." Yet, I quickly discovered that in practice, they did neither. A very demanding dissident shareholder was driving them to under-invest in the business and emphasize short-term profitability over long-term investment in people and relationships. When I pointed this out to them, there was consternation and defensiveness. Over time, however, I was able to make a dent and they began reallocating more budget toward people development.

## Two tools for reframing

*Thoughtful questions* that explore the client's issue are one of your most potent tools to help reframe. A very simple opener could be, "What else in your organization must fall into place in order for this initiative to be a success?"

Other questions could:

- Probe higher-level business goals
- Explore cross-functional and enterprise-wide implications
- Challenge the client's framing of the problem
- Ask about alignment with strategy and requirements for implementation success
- Explore underlying assumptions
- And so on . . .

A second powerful tool is *metaphor.* A metaphor is a figure of speech that illuminates something else. For example, I had a client who kept chasing too many small clients. As a result, they couldn't grow. I shared a metaphor with them which I also mentioned on Day 1 of this book: "A lioness cannot live on a diet of mice alone. You just can't catch enough of them to stay healthy!" They got the point.

In 1939, President Franklin D. Roosevelt created a powerful reframing of the need for the United States to help the British defend themselves against Nazi Germany. At the time, the US congress was isolationist and did not want to get involved in the growing European conflict. Nazi leader Adolf Hitler, however, began massing his forces to lay siege to Britain. The British desperately needed American help. A major obstacle stood in Roosevelt's way: After World War I, a series of laws had been passed in Congress that put restrictions on armament sales to foreign governments.

At a news conference, Roosevelt said, in referring to the need to help the British, "If your neighbor's house was on fire, wouldn't you lend them your garden hose to help put it out?" Everyone understood exactly what he was saying. This immediately helped engage public opinion around the need to help our British "neighbors."

Roosevelt then got Congress to accept the Lend-Lease program, which circumvented the restrictions and was instrumental in helping Britain fend off the German air assault known as "The Blitz."

Where you sit is often where you stand. A corporate manager will usually define problems from his or her own particular perspective—and that may lead to the challenge being underestimated. Your job is to ensure the right problem has been identified and the best, highest-impact solution is being pursued.

**PUTTING KEY IDEAS INTO ACTION**

- Think about a business development discussion you're having right now with a client. Work through the "compass" points to identify opportunities to reframe the issue as presented to you by the client:
  - North into strategy
  - South into implementation
  - East into enterprise-wide implications
  - West into change management
- Either for the same issue or one that you're discussing with another client, can you think of opportunities for a more radical reframing of the issue? For example:
  - Highlight opposites
  - Reprioritize
  - Challenge assumptions
  - Identify the root cause
  - Expose the inconsistency of their beliefs

# Week 9 Grow Your Relationships: The 10-Minute Plan

A law firm I advised had a long-standing client that was one of the world's largest corporations. Every year, the chairman of the law firm asked the partner in charge of the account how things were going. "Great, we have a terrific relationship," he inevitably told the chairman. This company had, after all, been a client of the firm for decades. But something insidious was happening: each year, the firm's revenues from this client shrunk. Even though this was a full-service, global law firm, their business with the client had diminished to just a few engagements. As a result, they were no longer on the General Counsel's radar—they had ceased being strategic for the client.

Yes, at the end each year this client still went in the "retained" column, and there was inevitably some light applause for the partner in charge of it. But the relationship was a shadow of its former self.

The new retention is *expansion.* If you're not growing a client relationship in some way, you may very well be backsliding into irrelevance. If you aren't broadening your footprint and impact, you are effectively losing ground.

Put another way, if you aren't one of a client's top two or three advisors or suppliers in your area of expertise—or on your way to becoming one of them—then you risk becoming increasingly irrelevant. You're a vendor to be "managed," and, when times are tough, cut.

This week, I'll share with you a 10-minute plan that will help you grow your client relationships. Ten minutes? Really? Yes, because the framework of eight questions I use can literally be reviewed in as little as ten minutes. Usually, though, I'd recommend you engage with them for a few hours. At the other extreme, I've done planning off-sites with clients where we took *three days* to go through these same questions for a single large account! These questions are like an accordion. You can expand or contract the time devoted to them according to your needs and time constraints.

## The power of focus

Why do some client relationships thrive and grow, while others wither on the vine? Understanding the answer is pretty important, because client growth drives enterprise growth. I've been studying this question for years, and have worked with well over 100 leading companies in the B2B (business-to-business) space on the challenge of relationship growth.

The short answer is that, at the 10,000-foot level, there are two key drivers of growth: *potential* and *focus.* Maximizing potential is principally about choosing clients that are right for you. In Week 1, I set out three screening criteria for selecting clients: strategic fit, relationship fit, and potential impact. Quite simply, if you pick the right clients, growth comes more easily.

Here, I'll concentrate on the second driver—*focus.* Focus, if you've chosen the right clients, leads to growth.

Focus means, first of all, being client-centric. Some companies become internally focused, and they lose sight of why they are in business in the first place. As the great management sage Peter Drucker wrote, "The purpose of a business is to create and keep a customer."

I was once invited to work with a large professional services firm that had stopped growing. One of the first things I did was ask to see the time sheets for their top 10 executives. I wanted to understand how much time they were actually spending with clients each month, either on a billable or non-billable basis. The average was 1%, or around two hours a month for each leader. I sat in on executive committee meetings and noticed that they talked endlessly about internal policy, but rarely discussed clients. During one of these meetings, the CEO's assistant came in with a pink message slip—it was a client calling. He brushed it off and told her to take a message. That was the moment I knew, definitively, that they had lost their way. I told them that they needed to both improve their client development capabilities *and* establish new cultural behaviors and values.

Focus also means making your highest-potential relationships the center of your attention. This is why many companies segment their client base and provide differentiated service to the most promising accounts. As an individual consumer, you probably like the perks that can accompany being a "gold" customer or some similar designation. As a side note, this unfortunately has been carried to an absurd extreme by the airline industry. One airline I fly now has nine different classes of flyers and an absolute circus-like boarding process to match—it's all sizzle and no steak.

For a large organization, one of the best mechanisms to provide focus is a key client account management program. The data on the results of these programs is very encouraging. I typically see well-run key account programs achieving annual growth rates that are two or sometimes three times the growth that clients not in the programs achieve. In other words—as an illustration—if the average client growth rate for a firm is 5% per year, I'll often see the key accounts growing at 10 or 15% per year.

You might ask: But doesn't it become a self-fulfilling prophesy when you put your best clients in the program? Not really. These focus programs achieve more than just an illusionary or placebo effect (e.g., tell a client they're a key account, and even if nothing has changed, they give you more business). Some of my clients have tracked this. Often, they will see client accounts that have been stagnant for years suddenly take off like a rocket when they get the added attention and resources of a key account program.

Finally, focus should lead to targeted investments in growing your clients. With several of my clients I've developed formal investment programs for their most promising accounts. The key account manager or relationship partner is invited, each year, to design an investment plan for their client. This plan specifies activities to develop the relationship, and a desired budget.

### Mind share leads to wallet share

If *potential* and *focus* are key foundations of client relationship growth, gaining "mind share" is an essential, supporting strategy you should embrace. When you have mind share, you are influencing your client's agenda with your thought leadership. You are adding value above and beyond the service or product you sell. If you have low mind share and low wallet share, you're a niche vendor for your client. They will be unlikely to have much loyalty toward you.

If you have low wallet share, you don't grow it by "cross-selling," which often seems to mean simply showing up at your clients and pitching them on other services you offer. Rather, you do it by regularly adding value to your clients' understanding of their challenges and the potential solutions to address them. If you work with a firm, this also means introducing expert colleagues who can explore new areas with the client. When both mind share and wallet share are high, you're in a very strong position.

## Eight essential questions

For each of your significant clients, there are eight questions you need to answer. Think of this as a process rather than a one-off exercise. In order to properly respond to these questions, you will likely need to spend some time thinking on your own *and* talking to your client to get the required information.

### Question 1: What is your current position with this client?

Start by assessing your relationship with this client. I'm going to give you two ways to do this: One is quick-and-dirty and the other is comprehensive. To get ready for this step, you should print out your sales, other financial history, and contract/project history with the client over time. Also map out an organization chart and circle your key relationships.

The quick-and-dirty method is to rate each client (the account, not the individual executives) A, B, or C. This may sound like the segmentation framework I suggested in Week 3, but that was for a calling plan for both clients and prospects—a business development categorization. This is different.

An "A" client is one of your best clients. It's either a large current relationship or a small relationship that had very strong growth potential. All A clients will pass the three screens referenced in Week 1—strategic, relational, and impact.

A "B" client is a good, steady, bread-and-butter client. You have a good relationship, and things chug along. B clients probably think of you more as a "steady supplier"—a trusted expert—than a trusted advisor.

A "C" client is a question mark. C clients can be small clients of dubious economic value. They can also be large clients who treat you like a vendor, always pressure you on fees, and don't seem to want to have a trusted relationship with you.

### *The characteristics of a great relationship*

The more comprehensive method to evaluate your position with any given client is to assess each of the characteristics of a good relationship. Review Figure 9.1, which lists seven fundamental qualities of a strong relationship. Use this to rate your client relationships. You might find that it uncovers some important gaps that need your attention.

Overall, how would you summarize the state of this relationship? Does the client view you as:

- An expert-for-hire/vendor?
- A trusted advisor?
- A trusted partner? (This is when you have built multiple trusted-advisor relationships across the client's company and they buy a wide range of services or products from your firm.)

## SEVEN CHARACTERISTICS OF HEALTHY CLIENT RELATIONSHIPS

| | |
|---|---|
| 1. **Trust.** There is strong trust in our relationship, enabling us to work informally and without frequent checking or micromanagement. | Never Always<br>1 2 3 4 5 |
| 2. **Value.** This client perceives very strong value-added from our work together. | Never Always<br>1 2 3 4 5 |
| 3. **Respect.** The client carefully listens to what we have to say and respects us as people and as professionals. | Never Always<br>1 2 3 4 5 |
| 4. **Transparency.** The client communicates frequently and openly shares their plans and priorities with us. | Never Always<br>1 2 3 4 5 |
| 5. **Loyalty.** In my area of expertise, this client will always speak to me first about a need they have. | Never Always<br>1 2 3 4 5 |
| 6. **Financial Performance.** This relationship meets our expectations for absolute levels of revenue and profitability, as well as for revenue growth. | Never Always<br>1 2 3 4 5 |
| 7. **Reference-ability.** If asked, this client would provide an enthusiastic testimonial or a referral to someone they know. | Never Always<br>1 2 3 4 5 |

**Figure 9.1** The seven characteristics of healthy client relationships

Last: What is your biggest, single challenge in growing this relationship? I find it helpful to boil all of the issues you may have down to the one, singular obstacle that you need to overcome.

## Question 2: What are your aspirations?

Most great entrepreneurs dream big. Billionaire Richard Branson, who now controls over 400 companies, has always had ambitious aspirations for his business ideas. When he started the recording label Virgin Records in 1972, it was nothing more than small recording studio he had built in his country house in Oxford. Yet, he confidently went after the best and most interesting music talent, later signing groups like the Rolling Stones and the Sex Pistols. More recent ventures include Virgin Galactic, which modestly aspires to create a space tourism business and launch satellites into orbit. In his autobiography, Branson writes, "My interest in life comes from setting myself huge, apparently unachievable challenges and trying to rise above them . . . from the perspective of wanting to live life to the full, I felt that I had to attempt it."

The most successful rainmakers, whether they are solo practitioners or work with a firm, think like entrepreneurs. They set very high goals for their client relationships. They aren't content to robotically project 5 or 10% growth each year. They aim at no less than becoming their clients' most important provider in their area of expertise.

Think about one of your most important clients. What are your aspirations? Consider factors such as:

- Client impact
- Revenue and profitability
- Share of wallet
- Relationship quality
- Level of the organization you work with

### Question 3: What is the client's agenda?

In Week 7 ("Anticipate and Agenda Set") I set out the concept of your client's *agenda.* Let's elaborate more on this, because it's such a critical ingredient of relationship growth.

There are several levels and types of agendas. First, there is the corporate or institutional agenda. What are your client's three to five most important strategies or goals, at the firm level?

Second, each executive you work with has a professional agenda. This comprises their three to five most important priorities, needs, or goals that should—ideally—flow from the institutional agenda.

Third, everyone has a personal agenda. These priorities could range from managing their careers to dealing with a family crisis. This is relevant not because you're trying to be a therapist but because if you want to be a trusted advisor to your clients, you need to understand them *as people.*

I've worked with hundreds of teams on account planning, and this question—what is the client's agenda?—trips almost everyone up. Many of my clients can sketch out the corporate agenda, but few—*very few*—have a thorough knowledge of the agendas of the individual executives they work with.

### Question 4: What are the best opportunities for growing the relationship?

Given where you are starting from (question 1), what your aspirations are (question 2), and the client's priorities and goals (question 3), in which areas can you can add value to your client through a solution you offer?

In Week 6, I introduced the concept of *growth catalysts.* Keep these in mind as you think through this question. What external challenges do your clients face, in terms of competition, the economy, customer trends, and so on? Where do they wish they were moving faster? What capability gaps are they trying to fill? If a new CEO or other top executive has taken over, what is their agenda and how will that affect the area you work with?

In response to this question, you should be able to write down at least three or four opportunities that you can explore with your client.

### Question 5: What individual relationships need to be deepened?

My own clients, especially those that serve large accounts, often spend the most time answering this question. And they are the most frustrated by it. You'd think it would be easy.

The easy part is making a list of executives and saying, "We need to build a relationship with these individuals in order to grow the account." The list should include the executives you need to work with for the current engagement, *and* the executives who would be the future clients for additional solutions you could offer.

The hard part is figuring out exactly how to develop those relationships. There are three main barriers:

- It takes hard work to build a relationship with someone. There's no silver bullet—as I said earlier, it's like diet and exercise.
- Because we don't understand the other person's priorities, needs, and goals—his or her agenda—we don't quite know where to start.
- Sometimes, there is simply a lack of understanding of how relationships are developed in the first place.

At this point in our 100-day journey, I want to introduce a very simple relationship-building model. You may already be a pro at this. Or maybe not. Remember my global survey of nearly 3,000 professionals just like you? Only 30% said they were *highly* satisfied with their professional relationships (the rest were somewhat satisfied or not satisfied with them).

This process works for any professional relationship you want to build, whether with clients or your manager. Figure 9.2 shows what it looks like.

When you first meet someone, you build rapport and get to know one another. Then, you work to understand the person's agenda—what's important to him or her. Next, you try to add value to that agenda. As the relationship progresses, you get to know him or her more deeply as a person. And you stay in touch over time. As you go through these steps, trust slowly develops and strengthens.

So you've made your list of key executive relationships that you want to develop. Now you need to emulate the client I described in Week 7—the one who carried that little slip of paper, with his clients' goals listed, around in his pocket. For each executive on your list, write down the person's three to five most important professional priorities, needs, or goals. Then do the same for their personal agendas.

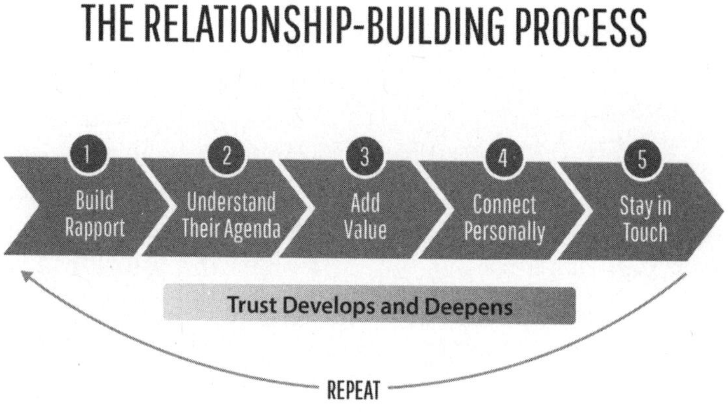


**Figure 9.2** The relationship-building process

My guess is that if you're like many of my clients, you will struggle to complete this exercise in one sitting because you don't know the agenda of these individuals. So this is your homework and next step: meet with your clients, one by one, and start really learning about what's important to them. I don't mean what's important to them around your existing contract. I'm talking about their overall agenda of critical priorities, needs, and goals.

As the CEO of a $15 billion corporation said to me, "Even when I was a mid-level manager, I never had a client say 'no' when I called them up and said, 'I'd like to drop by and buy you a cup of coffee, and gain a better understanding of your plans and priorities.'"

**CLIENT ACCOUNT PLANNING BEST PRACTICES**

- Concentrate on the quality of your thinking, not the form.
- Involve your client in designing your plan.
- Deliver on what the client has asked you do in the first place.
- Identify the buying influences.
- Understand rational, political, and personal agendas.
- Think about—and revisit it regularly—how you are adding value.
- Strategize how to increase your share of mind.
- Ask yourself and your team lots of tough questions.
- Conduct an independent client review.
- Get an objective, honest broker to participate in the planning process.
- Convert your plan to specific action steps and monitor progress.
- Review and adapt your plan on an ongoing basis.

## Question 6: What investments can and should you make?

We sometimes forget that there is an "I" in ROI—the *investment* part of "return on investment." A vegetable garden doesn't thrive just because you throw some seeds on the ground and return months later. I tried that last summer. In late May I planted a bunch of tomato and squash seedlings in the rear garden of our home in the southwest, and then left for six weeks. When my wife and I returned, the plants had been reduced to scarred, brown stumps. Rabbits, insects, and deer had devastated them in my absence. It looked like a Biblical plague of locusts had struck. Similarly, client relationships don't prosper without steady investment and cultivation over a long period of time.

There are two types of "agenda setting" investments you can make. The first is what I would call *daily thought leadership.* Based on your understanding of your client's agenda of key priorities, you develop ideas, perspectives, points of view, and useful information that will add value to that agenda.

I had a client, for example, who felt her organization did not have a culture of accountability. Specifically, she wanted people to take more responsibility for solving problems instead of pointing to her and saying, "This needs fixing." I was working on a different issue for this client, but gave some thought to her cultural challenge. One day, we had coffee together, and I suggested she take a look at the modern-day versions of the old GE "Work-Out" methodology. Since I've been around for a while, I have the advantage of remembering some good management ideas that were very effective years ago but have since lost visibility. I walked her through the idea of creating small working groups that would be empowered to tackle vexing issues such as slow decision making or wasteful spending. She liked the idea a lot and eventually came up with her own version of GE's "Work-Out" process, tailored to her organization.

A second type of investment is a more substantial one—let's call it *the deep dive.* I had a large client, with substantial resources, who was thinking about expanding their use of eLearning in their training programs. They had reviewed, and liked, my own eLearning courses on building clients for life. However, they wanted everything customized to their particular business and culture. But they weren't ready to make a commitment to do anything yet.

I invested significant time to produce a demo lesson that was highly tailored for them. It included examples of how their own executives had used the relationship-building strategies and techniques that I talked about in the sample. A few months later, impressed with the demo, they hired me to create a program just for them. Without that investment, it's unlikely I could have persuaded them. Sometimes, you have to show your client what they are going to get—describing it on a PowerPoint slide isn't enough. It's like showing someone a photograph of a delicious meal versus letting him actually sample the food.

On a larger scale, one of my clients, a leading consulting firm, aspired to work for a major Fortune 100 company. It was a hard nut to crack, however—this company virtually never used outside advisors. My client decided to go for broke. They sent a senior partner to actually live in the small headquarters city of this company, and for nearly a year he met with executives at the company, getting to know them and trying to understand their issues. It wasn't easy: nearly every meeting started the same way. Each executive he met with would welcome him by saying, "You know, we just don't use consultants around here!" He finally got a small project. And then another. Four years later, it had grown to become a $100 million per year client!

---

**Based on the scale of the potential opportunities, and your own resources and priorities, what investments can you make in your clients?**

---

## Question 7: What resources do you need?

Strategy development methodologies used to be premised on how a company could optimize limited resources in the pursuit of its goals. This thinking was somewhat upended when Gary Hamel and C. K. Prahalad developed their concept of "strategic intent." They maintained that highly successful companies didn't simply set goals based on how much gas they had in their tank. Rather, they set bold aspirations and then went out and *acquired* the resources they needed to achieve them. To some extent this is what Apple did when it developed the first iPhone. They procured a large variety of existing technologies, supported by a global supply chain that their current CEO had helped build, and integrated them into a mobile phone.

Decide on how far you want to travel, and then procure the means necessary for the trip.

For this step in your client growth planning, you need to make a wish list of the people, skills, resources, money, and other assets you need to achieve the ambitious goals you set when you answered Question 2 about your aspirations for the relationship. In other words, take a *strategic intent* approach to growing your client relationships, not one based on a "closed system" of limited resources.

In practice, what does this mean? If you work with a large firm, you need to identify resources across your organization that could potentially be marshaled in support of your client plan. These could include colleagues who are subject matter experts, systems or processes that will help manage the relationship, thought leadership and research in areas of interest to your client, budget to invest in "deep dives," and so on. You can formalize this by creating a fund that gives client account teams investment money to direct toward growth ideas.

What about if you're a solo practitioner or have a small firm? You may feel you don't have access to the resources necessary to drive the aspirational growth I'm highlighting. Here's what I do:

- I carefully make decisions about where to invest my time and money. Focus = growth, so I concentrate on the highest-potential clients in making these major agenda-setting investments.
- I work to produce lots of ideas that I share with my clients. My ideas cost me nothing except a little reflection time. I don't pre-judge these ideas because I never know exactly which ones will resonate. Sometimes clients think they are great, and sometimes they just say "hmm" and move on. Occasionally, what I thought was just a little idea is, for the client, a very big one—and vice versa. You never know.
- I also like to collect ideas. I take careful notes of all of my conversations and try to capture any insights or new perspectives that arise. I also read widely, often outside my area of expertise, and scan a lot of books and articles. When I do this, I'm looking at information through the lens of the different executives I'm working with. I ask myself, "Is this something that is relevant for one of my clients?" And if so, I'll pass it on.
- I have a network of other professionals who are experts in a variety of fields and specialties. I try to make myself available to them if they need help or advice, and I also occasionally call on them when I need expert input on an issue. Sometimes, I introduce these individuals and their firms to my clients when there is a need I can't fulfill.

These are some of the practices that help me "punch above my weight" as a small firm.

### Question 8: What is your plan?

What's left now is to make a list of action steps to implement your growth plan. These will naturally fall out of your answers to the previous seven questions. You should specify the task, when you plan to accomplish it, and who is going to do it if it's someone other than you.

## No plan survives contact with the client

You control many of the important factors that will determine whether a client relationship thrives or declines. You're in charge of how often you go to see your clients, the agenda-setting investments you make, the value for time you add in your conversations, the quality of your delivery, and so on. Sure, some clients are tougher than others, but don't throw your hands up in the air in despair. If a relationship seems like a constant uphill struggle—even a dead end—move on and apply your talents to a different client.

Finally, be intentional and focused, but also flexible. Helmuth von Moltke (1800–1891) was a Prussian field marshal who is considered a modern military genius. He famously wrote, "No battle plan ever survives contact with the enemy." I've borrowed this phrase and changed it to "No plan survives contact with the client." Do your homework and develop a growth plan for your client. But once you start engaging with them around the ideas in that plan, the conversation may go to unexpected places. So be flexible and adapt to conditions on the ground.

**PUTTING KEY IDEAS INTO ACTION**

Pick a current client relationship that has strong potential. Answer the eight questions to help you develop a growth plan for it.

1. What is your current position with this client?
2. What are your aspirations?
3. What is the client's agenda?
4. What are the best opportunities for growing the relationship?
5. What individual relationships need to be deepened, and how will you strengthen them?
6. What investments can and should you make?
7. What resources do you need?
8. What is your plan?

# Week 10 Use Power Questions

A client of mine met with a managing director at a large private equity firm. The firm was racing to divest a company it owned. "We're in a rush," he told my client. "I want only one, very specific project done." After exploring that opportunity, my client suggested some additional work that would enhance the project's success. But the managing director waved his hand and said no.

My client then asked him a simple but transformative question: "I'm curious, if you *did* have more time before selling this company, what else, *ideally*, would you fix in order to make it more valuable to buyers?"

The executive paused, and reflected in silence. He finally spoke: "Hmm . . . well . . . actually, there are also two other problems I'd probably address." He briefly described them. There was more silence. Then he added, "Ok, please put them in your proposal as well."

The question instantly shifted the discussion and considerably changed the focus of the work. The client went from wanting to pay the least fees possible for a small project to agreeing to a broad scope of work that would dramatically increase the value of the asset.

If you aspire to be a trusted advisor to your clients, you have to get better at asking thought-provoking questions. I call them *Power Questions.* In talking about their most important external providers, many senior executives have mentioned this skill to me. The CEO of a Fortune 500 corporation once told me: "I can always tell how experienced a potential provider is by the quality of their *questions.*" Note that he didn't say, "because of how clever they are" or "because of the quality of their PowerPoint slides."

In the same vein, the great artist Picasso quipped, "Computers are useless. They can only give you answers."

Since I co-authored the global bestseller *Power Questions* with the late, great Jerry Panas (that's him in the illustration!), I've worked hard to improve the quality of my own questions. The results have been more than encouraging—they've been exhilarating. One type of question that I particularly like, which I'll explore later, focuses on the realm of the *emotions.* It's a personal question that draws out emotion, passion, and enthusiasm. Let me illustrate what I mean.

A few years ago, I spoke at the annual executive offsite for a large corporation. Afterward, I was invited to hear the CEO's state-of-the-firm speech. He presented for about 20 minutes, and then asked if there were any questions. Hands shot up among the 150 top executives in the audience. The questions, however, were pedantic, nitpicky, and backward-looking ("Why are the financial reserves cited on slide 15 so high?"). The CEO became bored and deflated by the picayune questions.

So I raised my hand. "Bill, I'm curious—of all the initiatives you have going on, what are you personally most excited about?" He smiled, and then waxed enthusiastically for nearly five minutes about a very special project he was deeply passionate about. Afterward, as we were all leaving the auditorium, he approached me from behind and grabbed my shoulder. "Great question, Andrew," he shouted over the background din. "A very revealing question." He walked away, but then suddenly paused and turned around, adding: "Give me a call." I did, and that was the start of what became a great, long-term relationship with him and his company.

Good questions help clients see their problems in a new light. They engage the other person and draw them out. They help you get to the root cause of issues. They surface the really important aspects of the situation. The right question can even transform a relationship.

## What separates good questions from mediocre ones?

What is the difference between a good question and an average or poor one? Here are six characteristics of Power Questions:

- *They're usually open-ended.* They invite discussion, not a yes-or-no answer. Instead of "Are you concerned about the new regulations?" ask, "How are you being impacted by the new regulations?"
- *They are fresh and even surprising.* They make the other person stop and think. Drop clichéd questions

like "What keeps you up at night?" More interesting would be "What gets you up in the morning?"

- *They focus the conversation on the right issues, and in particular, on what the client is interested in.* Try asking, "What's the most important issue you'd like to discuss this morning?"
- *They help you get to the bigger picture.* Sometimes it's a "Why?" question. When you ask, "Why have you decided to launch this initiative now?" you move the conversation up a level. During Week 8, I mentioned the "five whys" used by Toyota founder Sakicho Toyoda to diagnose quality problems.
- *They help you uncover important information about the other person.* I sometimes invite clients to talk about their careers by asking questions like, "How did you get your start?" or "I'm curious, as you think about your career, what has your most important leadership experience been, and what did you learn?"
- *They can create buy-in* and *ownership.* If you make a declaration like, "We believe your customer response times are below industry standards," you will often create resistance and defensiveness. Whereas the question, "How do you feel about your response times?" creates engagement. If you do this—turn statements into questions—the other person will sometimes step up and admit, "We're not where we should be." Then you're off to the races.

## Four types of power questions

You can use many different types of power questions. Your selection will depend on the circumstances and your objectives. That said, to help you focus, I'd like to share a simple framework that many of my clients have found extremely helpful. I call it the *Power Questions Matrix.* It illustrates four directions you can take your questions.

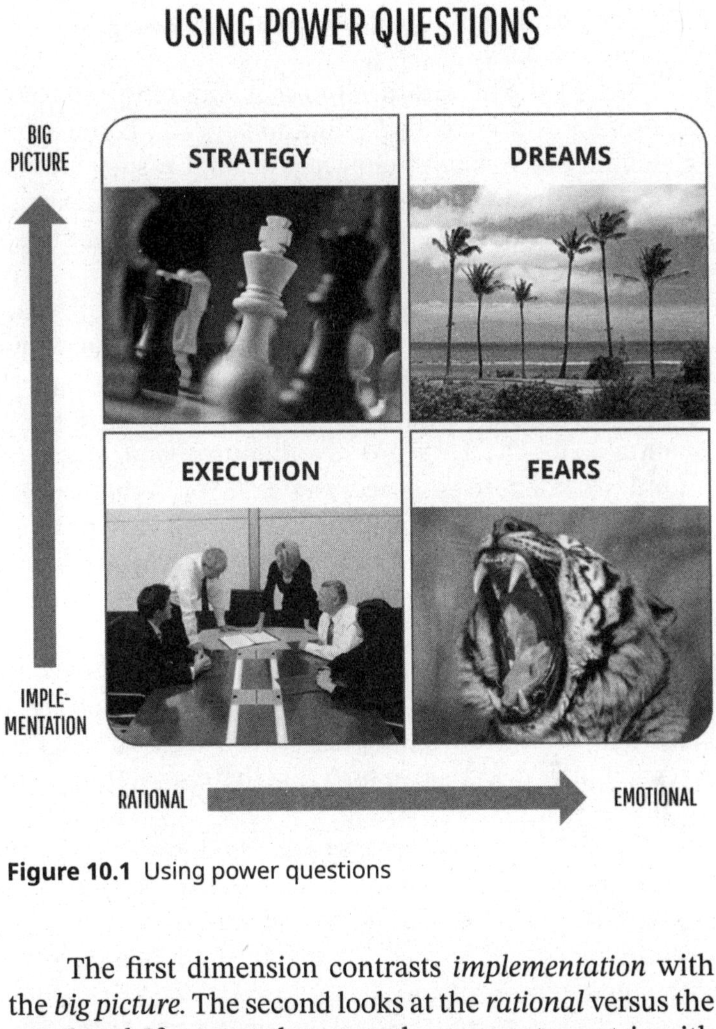


**Figure 10.1** Using power questions

The first dimension contrasts *implementation* with the *big picture*. The second looks at the *rational* versus the *emotional*. If you put these together, you get a matrix with four quadrants, as shown in Figure 10.1.

In the lower-left *execution quadrant*, you'll ask rational or analytical questions about how something is going to be implemented. These could be as simple as, "How do you plan to do that?" "What is your timing?" or "Which areas of the organization will be affected by this?" For most of my clients, this is the most comfortable quadrant.

It allows them to stay within their expertise and delve into the details.

But often, you also need to move up to the strategy quadrant in order to really understand the context for what your client is trying to accomplish. Let's say a prospect asks you how you would approach solving a particular problem. You need to answer the question, but to do so may require asking strategy questions.

In the upper-left *strategy quadrant*, you're still focused on rational or analytical questions, but now you're talking about the big picture. You might ask questions to get at higher-level goals, such as "Why do you want to do that?" "How are you aligning the priorities in your department to your new strategy?" or "What part of your strategy is this particular initiative supporting?"

As I mentioned in Week 8 on reframing, facts tell and emotions sell. So you must also understand the emotional or personal side of the issue. In the upper-right *dreams quadrant*, you might ask questions like, "What legacy do you hope to leave here?" "What are you working on right now that you're most excited about?" or "You've achieved so much in your career so far . . . is there something else you'd like to accomplish?"

Finally, in the lower-right *fears quadrant* you need to ask questions about concerns, anxieties, and frustrations—things that could get in the way of dreams and aspirations. For example, "As you think about your implementation program, what do you wish were going faster?" "What do you think is the biggest risk to this initiative?" or "Which aspects of our proposal do you have concerns or questions about?"

## More power questions

The Power Questions Matrix will help you, in any situation you find yourself, focus questions in the four quadrants of Execution, Strategy, Dreams, and Fears. Now let's look at some questions you can use at different stages of relationship-building.

### MY FAVORITE QUESTIONS

There are so many good questions that it's hard to boil them down to just a few. Four that I particularly like are:

- "What did you learn from that experience?" We often don't bother to stop and think, and this question creates space to do that.
- "Is this the best you can do?" Apple co-founder Steve Jobs used to ask this question frequently of his engineers, reflecting his unquenchable zeal for great, well-designed products.
- "Can we start over?" If you find yourself in the middle of a heated argument with a family member or friend, this can be a lifesaver. It allows you to hit the "reset" button and start again, calmly.
- "What are you working on that you're especially excited about?" I love hearing about what people are most passionate and enthusiastic about.

## Building rapport

Remember, rapport is driven by your client's perception of your trustworthiness, competence, and likeability. Showing an interest in the other person, finding things you have in common, asking thoughtful questions, adding value in the conversation, and being enthusiastic about your work will all contribute to positive rapport. I usually start with fairly safe questions that are unlikely to touch on any personal sensitivities. It's ok to start with the weather, but I would quickly shift to more meaningful topics.

Here's just small sample of rapport-building questions:

1. I saw in your bio that you graduated from xx . . . my brother went there—how was your experience?
2. I notice you spent a couple of years at xyz corporation . . . I actually started my career there in the late 90s. How did you find your time there?

3. I'm curious, where do you live? Do you have much of a commute? Did you grow up in this area?
4. Can you tell me something about your own career and how you got to your current role?
5. How would you compare the experience of working here versus at your old organization?
6. I understand you've worked here for nearly xx years. I'm curious, what are some of the biggest changes you've seen since you joined?
7. So what do you think about . . . (a current event, trend, some breaking news, etc.)?
8. What passions or hobbies do you enjoy outside of work?

### Exploring the client's issues

These are some of the questions I like to use to better understand someone's issues. They can work equally well whether it's a prospect or a new executive you're meeting at a current client's.

1. From your perspective, what would be the most valuable way for us to spend this time together? (or "What issues do you want to make sure we discuss today?")
2. What are your aspirations for your business two to three years out?
3. What organizational and operational capabilities do you need to support those aspirations?
4. What are the gaps in your capabilities, between what you have today and what you feel you need to support your strategy?
5. In talking to my other clients in your industry, I'm struck by three particular issues they are grappling with. These include . . . (list them). How would these resonate with you and your management?
6. How is your organization reacting to . . . (a recent, important development in this client's industry or function)?

7. What are your most significant opportunities for growth over the next several years?
8. In what areas do you wish you were moving faster?
9. How would you describe the biggest challenges facing your customers?
10. How will you and your area be evaluated at the end of the year?

### Delving deeper into an identified need

Once a client has zeroed in on an important, urgent issue that you might potentially collaborate around, you can explore it more deeply. Here are some questions that will be helpful to do that:

1. How much do you think this problem is costing you?
2. What's the revenue growth potential presented by this opportunity?
3. How is this affecting other aspects of your business (sales, costs, productivity, customer satisfaction, employee morale, etc.)?
4. If you do not address this (problem/opportunity), how might your business be impacted?
5. How do you know that . . . (turnover is high, productivity is low, risks are not being well managed, etc.)?
6. Why is this particularly important to you right now?
7. Would you say this is one of your top three or four priorities?
8. What solutions have you already tried, and how successful were they?

### Gaining feedback from your clients

Clients generally don't voice their concerns with you. Instead, they tend to vote with their feet, gradually and often invisibly shifting their business to a competitor. So you need to seek feedback on a regular basis.

These questions will help you understand the state of your relationship:

1. Could you share with me your overall assessment of our relationship?
2. If you could change or improve one thing about our relationship, what would it be?
3. Are there any individuals in your organization with whom we should invest more time and build a better relationship?
4. Can you give me any suggestions for improving the amount, timing, or format of our communications to you and your organization?
5. What issues are coming up that we ought to be aware of or thinking about for you?
6. What are your plans for . . . ? How are you planning to deal with . . . ? (Tailor these to your client's business and markets.)
7. What are your most important goals over the next six to 12 months?
8. Is there anything we could improve upon or change that would make doing business with us easier?
9. Could you give me your assessment of our team? What have they done particularly well? What could they do better?
10. Would you be willing to provide us with a referral or testimonial?

## Questions you should never ask

You've probably heard this expression before: "There are no bad questions." Well, please forget you ever heard it. There are *plenty* of bad questions out there, and I don't want you asking them!

Of course, the appropriateness and ultimate value of a question can vary depending on when and how it is used. In other words, the worth of a question is not absolute. For example, "Why?" can be an excellent question, as in "I'm curious, why have you decided to launch this initiative now?" or "Why do you think people are not taking advantage of your new account planning tool?" But a "why" question could also come across as critical and carping if used in the wrong way. For example, never ask, "Why did you do that?" after someone has made a mistake—the real message is, "Why were you so stupid?"

Here are eight questions you should rarely or never ask:

1. *What keeps you up at night?* If you're meeting for the first time with a prospective client, this is a lazy question that shows you haven't done any homework or preparation for a meeting. It's also a cliché, in that salespeople have been asking it for last 25 years. You've got to be more creative than that. With an old friend or client you've known for years, you might ask this—but not with a prospect.
2. *What has surprised you?* This is often asked of someone who recently took over a new job. It's a poor question because there is no good answer. If someone tells you "nothing," then he risks coming across as overconfident and unaware. If she tells you she was "surprised" by a bunch of things, then she appears to have been un-informed and unprepared for the role. Instead, ask, "Have you identified your longer-term priorities yet?" or "How have you focused your time during these first few months?"
3. *What question haven't I asked you?* That's an old salesman's trick, to get your prospect into the position of being your coach and sitting, in effect, on the same side of the table. "We're in this together!" But sophisticated executives see right through that one. Ask instead, "Are there any other issues we haven't discussed that you think are relevant to this topic?"

4. *What would it take to get your business?* (Ouch.) I still see this question in books on selling. You get someone's business by building a relationship of trust and demonstrating that your product or service can add value and solve a problem—not by asking this crude question. The client's answer, by the way, just might be, "Well, if you cut your price by 50% that would help."
5. *If I could show you a way to save a substantial amount of money, would you be interested in a proposal from us?* This is an old and unappetizing chestnut used by desperate salespeople who are missing their targets. Please—you insult the other person's intelligence when you ask something like this.
6. *What does success look like?* On the surface, this isn't a terrible question at all. But it's a red-hot cliché! I've seen senior client executives roll their eyes and sigh when asked this question. It would be better if you just rearranged the words: "How will you know if you've succeeded?" I prefer to ask this in a slightly different way: "What are the measures of success you'll be looking for in a year's time?" or "If you successfully solve this challenge, what will be different in a year's time?"
7. *Would 10 a.m. Monday work for a call to discuss our new megalith solution?* How do you feel when salespeople try this line on you? If you're selling steak knives, it might be a good way secure an appointment. But if you sell high-end products and services, forget it. Some readers may disagree with me on this one. However, I maintain you shouldn't use it if you aspire to be a trusted expert or trusted advisor to senior executives.

Finally—and a lot of people ask their clients this question:

8. *How can we add more value to you?* Most of the time, clients cannot answer that question. They either mumble something like, "Keep up the good work" or "Please don't mess this project up." *You* have to

figure out how you can do a better job for them. You do this by spending time with your clients, learning their business, and understanding their frustrations, needs, goals, and priorities. Only *you* can make the connection between those client needs that you perceive and your particular product or service. Don't expect your clients to put the two together—they rarely will. There are many better questions you can ask that will help you understand how to do a better job (e.g., see my previous list of questions to help you get client feedback).

## Ask, don't tell

I'm going to end Week 10 by giving you four important principles about asking questions.

### Principal one: Turn statements into questions

Sometimes, a clear judgment is called for and you have to express your opinion very directly. But often, framing an issue within a question ("How do you feel about . . . ?") is more engaging. This draws your clients out rather than making them retreat defensively, like hermit crabs, withdrawing into their shells.

### Principal two: Don't ask too many questions

I got a call once from a prospective client who had read *Power Questions*. Here's how the conversation went:

*Client:* "You know," he told me, in a slightly reprimanding, I-told-you-so tone of voice, "I tried your questioning technique and it didn't work."

*Me:* "Really? What happened?"

*Client:* "The client told me after the meeting that I had asked way too many questions, and that it got tedious for her."

*Me:* "How many questions did you ask?"

*Client:* "I went in with a list of around 25 questions."

Twenty-five is a numbingly large number of questions to ask someone in a business development conversation. I can usually run a one-hour meeting with just a few well-chosen questions. Don't act like you're cross-examining your client in court or interviewing him or her for a job!

### Principal three: Be confident and relaxed

If you are nervous, insecure, and feel the other person is going to be offended, your question may very well come across as rehearsed and inauthentic. Relax and smile slightly when you ask a provocative question. Show warmth—doing so will help the other person also relax and be less defensive.

### Principal four: Bring three good questions to every client meeting

Start shifting some of your meeting preparation time into the development of power questions instead of fine-tuning your PowerPoint slides. It takes time and effort to come up with them, but the payoff is well worth it. If you bring three thoughtful questions to every client meeting, you will dramatically increase the quality and impact of your conversations.

**PUTTING KEY IDEAS INTO ACTION**

1. What is the most interesting and thought-provoking question you've ever been asked? Why was it helpful to you? What does that tell you about the kinds of questions that could be useful with your clients?

2. Think about an upcoming client meeting. Use the Power Questions Matrix to formulate a thoughtful question in each of the four quadrants—Execution, Strategy, Dreams, and Fears. Make it a goal to ask at least one or two of them.
3. Apply these questioning strategies, including the Power Questions Matrix, to your personal relationships with family and friends. What are some questions you'd like to ask the people closest to you?

**ADDITIONAL FREE RESOURCES FOR YOU**

Download my free *Client Growth Guide* at www.andrewsobel.com/growth-guide. It includes my Power Questions Toolkit, which will help you master the art and science of asking great, thought-provoking questions.

Week

# 11 Be a Brilliant Big-Picture Thinker

The summer before my senior year in high school, I attended a one-month program at the Minnesota Outward Bound School. I lived in New York City, and couldn't wait to get away from the sweltering heat—and my mother. Outward Bound offers wilderness programs that push you to your physical and mental limits. They are rewarding but very demanding experiences, perhaps even more so in that era.

For my "solo" experience I spent three days and three nights alone on the shore of a remote lake in the

Boundary Waters wilderness area. I had no food. I was given just three matches, a fishing hook, a rain tarp, and a metal cup. At night, nearby wolves howled nonstop as I huddled around a small fire.

One especially grueling segment of the course involved orienteering. In groups of three, we were dropped off in the wilderness. We had two days to hike, over difficult terrain, back to our instructors. They were waiting at a designated spot 10 miles away. To make the trekking even more difficult, they loaded our already-uncomfortable canvas packs with unneeded pots and pans to weigh us down.

Cell phones and portable GPS devices were still years in the future. So, armed with nothing more than terrain maps and a compass, our mission was to navigate to the pickup zone by sunset on day two. We had to traverse miles of swamps, thick forests, and steep ravines. The first night we camped next to a misty, gurgling bog. As the sun set, I remember the screen door of our tent slowly turning opaque from an encrustation of enormous, black mosquitoes that were trying to get inside to feed on us.

Of course, we got lost. Then, we couldn't find the main landmark, a rocky outcropping, that would guide us home. The expression, "Not seeing the forest for the trees" came vividly to life for me on that trip. We blindly stumbled along, covered in briar scratches and dozens of painful bug bites.

Despairing, I volunteered to shimmy up a tall tree on the top of a hill. As I got high enough to see the terrain around me, a cool breeze suddenly hit my face. Everything came into view. I could see where we had come from. I could also just spot the far-off clearing where our instructors waited, ahead of us. From that vantage point, I was able to pick out a perfect path for us to descend from the hill, and a river that would be easy to hike along. Four hours later—hungry, tired, and malodorous—we joyfully reunited with our two course leaders.

Today, whenever I feel a bit lost and in need of the bigger picture, I metaphorically try to climb back up that tall tree and see the panorama around me. With clients, it means pulling yourself out of the day-to-day details of the problems they face and seeing the larger context.

During this eleventh week of your 100-day plan, I'll give you proven strategies to climb your own tree and get the big picture for your clients. Hopefully, you won't need mosquito repellent, like I did, on your way up. First, I'll define what I mean by big-picture thinking. Then, I'll share a set of powerful techniques to gain broader perspectives and generate new ideas.

## What is big-picture thinking?

In the first phase of developing big-picture ideas for your clients, you start by learning about their overarching *goals.* What are they ultimately trying to accomplish? Next, you develop an understanding of the *total picture* or context around them. You climb a tree and take in the view. Finally, you identify the most *critical issues* that may affect the outcomes they seek. These three steps set you up for the second phase, which is idea development.

In the case of my youthful orienteering trek, the goal was to reach the meeting point by sunset of the second day. I finally obtained the total picture when I climbed the tree. I was able to gain a 360-degree understanding of the type of terrain around us. I could determine the approximate distance to our meeting point. The critical issues that I assessed were very practical factors: the physical condition of our team, the speed at which we could travel through the unmarked forest, the availability of drinkable water, and so on. These on-the-ground assessments actually led us to avoid the preferred route home that our instructors had suggested, instead heading to the river and then walking downstream.

With clients, don't underestimate the importance of being able to boil things down to these few, essential issues. I once led a consulting project for one of the largest retailers in the world. It was a complex assignment that assessed why their return on equity was underperforming and how to fix it. The final report was over 200 pages long and full of dense charts and tables. Just as we finished the engagement, a new CEO was installed. I sent the report to him, requesting a meeting. For six weeks I didn't hear back from him. I figured we were out of luck.

Then my phone rang on a Monday morning. It was the CEO himself. He was brief, and said, "You know, that report you sent me is pretty dense. Can you boil it down for us?" I struggled for a week to synthesize the document into five pages. But now, it contained precisely the essence of what we had discovered and were recommending. I highlighted the big-picture context of their competitive situation and customer trends. I also laid out three internal and three external factors that would impact the company's profitability going forward. Then I sent it to him.

A week later, the CEO called me again. "Thanks for the summary. Now I finally get it. By the way, I plan to circulate this summary to all my board members." That was the start of a long-term relationship. Later, he took to affectionately calling me "young Andrew" whenever we met, since at the time I was still in my early 30s.

## Ten strategies for generating new ideas

You've established your client's goals, gotten the total picture, and identified the critical issues or variables. Now, you now need to develop your specific ideas and frameworks to help your client achieve their goals and grow their business.

Here are ten techniques for creating new ideas and perspectives:

### 1. Develop simplifying frames.

A good, simplifying frame reduces many complex variables down to the most important two or three. It "frames up" key choices or positions. For example, years ago I developed a tool I call the Client Growth Matrix. I organized one of my books, *All for One*, around it. I still use it with great success with clients. Figure 11.1 shows what it looks like.

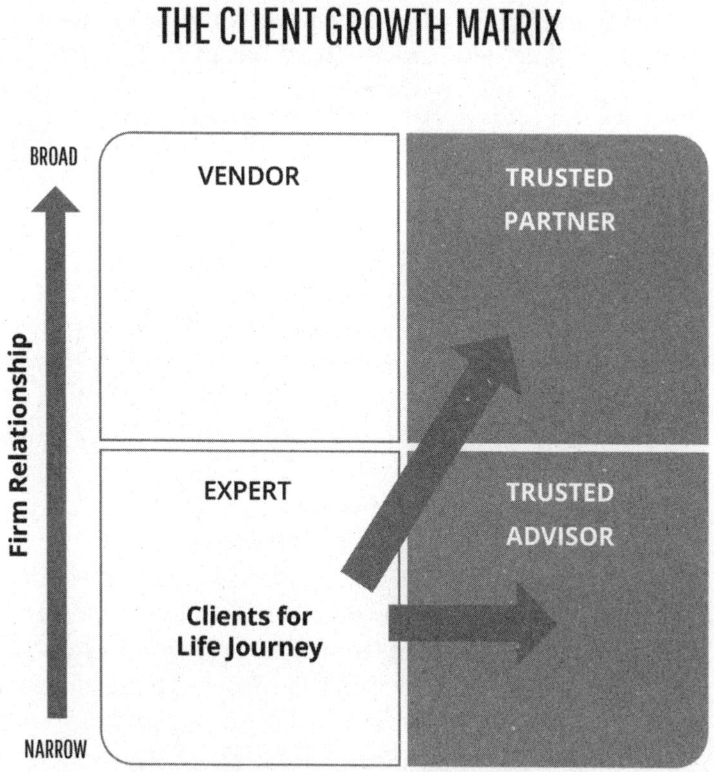


**Figure 11.1** The client growth matrix

I use this as a diagnostic tool with my clients, to help them assess their client relationships. I also use it during business development conversations. It helps spark a conversation about where clients are today and where they want to be in the future. We talk about barriers to getting to Trusted Partner and the capabilities of their team. The narrow versus broad scale on the Y axis refers both to the relative breadth of solutions (narrow versus broad) the client buys from you *and* the diversity of relationships you (and your organization) have established.

---

What kinds of simplifying frames could you develop for your clients, given the types of challenges they face?

---

## 2. Use metaphors and analogies

A metaphor is a figure of speech. It describes something in a way that isn't literally true, but which helps explain an idea or problem. In talking about innovation, an executive might say, "It's a marathon, not a sprint." This is a common business metaphor. Of course, innovation is not literally a "marathon," but the word illuminates the dynamics of successful long-term innovation.

A good metaphor can powerfully highlight or tee up an important idea and make it relatable to others. I mentioned this technique in Week 8, when I shared the story of President Franklin Roosevelt and his plea to help the British defend themselves from Hitler's Nazi advance. In that case, he compared helping the Brits to lending your garden hose to a neighbor whose house was on fire.

It's no coincidence that many great writers and artists are masters at using metaphor—it helps universalize their message. In *Romeo and Juliet*, Shakespeare doesn't write, "Juliet looked beautiful through the window"—which is literal. No, he penned something more powerful and transcendent: "But soft, what light through yonder window breaks? It is the east, and Juliet is the sun."

An analogy is a type of metaphor, but it is a more extensive, logical argument to compare two things. For example, I've often said that developing long-term client relationships is like nurturing a garden. You have to aerate and fertilize the soil, plant seeds, nurture the flowers and vegetables as they grow, pull out the weeds, and so on.

Marvin Bower, the individual most responsible for the modern-day development of the consulting firm McKinsey & Company, used a law firm analogy as the basis for the future culture he wanted to establish. In the 1940s, management consulting firms were looked on with skepticism (well, some things never change I suppose . . . !). Bower had previously worked for several years at the law firm of Jones, Day in Cleveland, and was impressed by their code of professional ethics and behavior. This became the driving force for him to professionalize McKinsey and imbue its culture with a similar set of standards of conduct.

---

For an upcoming client meeting, can you develop a powerful metaphor or analogy for your client?

---

### 3. Incorporate multiple perspectives

One illustration of this technique is the Balanced Scorecard approach to implementing strategy. It was developed in the early 1990s by Robert Kaplan and David Norton, and is widely used by corporations. The Balanced Scorecard looks at four perspectives: financial, customer/stakeholder, internal processes, and organization capacity (formerly learning and growth).

For your purposes, think about the different stakeholders or constituencies who will be affected in your work with clients. These will vary depending on where you are working in the organization. In my work, for example, I will often get the perspectives of:

- Senior management
- Human resources/learning and development
- Clients
- Client-facing professionals in sales, client management, client service, etc.

---

Are you missing some stakeholder perspectives in your client relationships?

---

### 4. Redefine the terms of the debate

Sometimes, it is possible to re-conceptualize a problem or situation by redefining the terms of the debate. I had a client who was being held back from promotion to a more senior leadership position because she didn't have experience managing large numbers of people. Historically, promotions at her company were justified by showing you had overseen more and more employees. But what the future leaders of her company needed was an entirely different set of skills. They had to be able to manage virtual, flexible workforces; cultivate alliance partners; and use digital technology more effectively.

I suggested she start talking, on every possible occasion, about the *new* leadership competencies of her organization. Her message was that the future of their business lay in developing a more flexible workforce and harnessing digital technologies to run the business. She insisted she be judged on her ability to do those things, not on whether or not she had experience in managing thousands of employees using the old command-and-control style. She reframed the debate, which helped secure her next promotion.

---

Could you help reset the assumptions about an important issue for one of your clients?

---

### 5. Look for patterns and commonalities

This technique was at the heart of the development of the so-called high-yield or "junk" bond market in the 1980s, which opened up financing to corporations that previously were shut out of the bond market. Drexel's Michael Milken obsessively studied the risk and returns of lower-rated bonds. He would pour over data on hundreds of bonds, even wearing a miner's headlamp on the train into work at 5 a.m., to better illuminate years of printouts. He found that low-rated, high-risk corporate bonds actually offered a risk-adjusted premium over high-rated, low-risk, blue-chip ones.

Another famous big-picture thinker who focused on *commonalities* was former secretary of state Henry Kissinger (also a controversial figure). He conceptualized the triangular balance of power among the US, the old Soviet Union, and China in the early 1970s. His starting point? The US and China had something important in common, which was the need to neutralize the Soviet Union's military and economic might. Others only saw irreconcilable differences between the US and China. His thinking led to Nixon's historic trip to China in 1972.

---

What patterns are you seeing, within your clients' business and also across all the clients you work with?

---

### 6. Suspend your judgment and even procrastinate

We admire decisiveness, but if you make up your mind too quickly, you risk closing out your best options. In his book, *Originals*, Wharton professor Adam Grant writes that many of the most creative thinkers procrastinate. He says, "Procrastination gives you time to consider divergent ideas, to think in nonlinear ways, to make unexpected leaps." One of the examples he cites is Martin Luther King Jr.'s famous "I Have a Dream" speech made on August 28, 1963. King was rewriting it right up to the end, with the phrase "I have a dream" penciled in at the very last minute. President Abraham Lincoln, similarly, made changes to his famous Gettysburg Address while traveling to the event on the train from the Capitol.

Perhaps you can recall a time you quickly made a decision, but later, wished you had waited to get more information or just reflect on the issue further. It requires a steady hand to wait until the last minute, but sometimes it pays off handsomely.

**ARE YOU BUILDING ON OTHERS' IDEAS?**

The singer-songwriter Bob Dylan spent years studying and absorbing a diverse range of folk music and African American spirituals before he wrote his folk-pop hits. And he very liberally borrowed melodies from those traditional songs for his own compositions. For example, his famous anthem "Blowin' in the Wind" borrows its melody from an African American slave spiritual called "No More Auction Block," and some of the words are adapted from the book of Ezekiel in the Bible. The great artist Pablo Picasso similarly developed new genres (such as Cubism) while liberally borrowing from many past traditions.

If you directly use someone else's idea, credit them. But don't be afraid to build on existing ideas to create something new or different. If a Dylan or Picasso can do it, so can you.

---

Do you ever rush to judgment about something or someone? Why do you think that happens?

---

## 7. Develop lots of ideas

This seems like a no-brainer. But many people, out of fear, don't develop their ideas and let them see the light of day. They don't share them with their clients or publish them. There's plenty of research showing that the most creative scientists—those who have won major awards—publish *lots* of articles. Most of their articles aren't acclaimed and don't win prizes. But some of them are and do, and that's what matters.

This applies in purely creative fields like musical composition. The play *Wicked* is the second-highest-grossing musical in history. Steven Schwartz, who wrote the music, has said, "There are 19 songs in *Wicked*, but I had to write 70 to get those 19."

In a more ordinary vein, on my own website there are well over 350 free articles, and I've written far more than that. I never know which ones are going to become popular or might become the idea for a full-length book. So I keep writing! Same with the videos I put out on YouTube. Some have had 10,000 views—others, a few hundred.

If I had been afraid of publishing content because I wasn't certain it would appeal to my audience, I would never have produced all my articles, videos, and books. Nor would I be where I am today.

---

Are you regularly developing ideas, writing them down, and getting them in front of your clients?

---

### 8. Connect and listen

One of the major findings of researchers who study the development of new ideas is that they rarely occur in a vacuum. Everyone loves the notion of the lone genius who has a eureka moment. But it's mostly a myth. According to innovation author Steven Johnson, new ideas almost always have their origins in a group or community. He describes how a researcher named Kevin Dunbar spent months observing and videotaping scientists at work. Johnson describes his work in a TED talk called *Where Good Ideas Come From*:

> . . . almost all of the important breakthrough ideas did not happen alone in the lab, in front of the microscope. They happened at the conference table at the weekly lab

> meeting, when everybody got together and shared their latest data and findings . . . [they] shared the mistakes they were making, the errors, the noise in the signal they were discovering. That . . . is the environment that leads to innovation.

Even in music composition, where there is certainly a lot of individual inspiration, Johnson's assertion holds some water. After the Beatles broke up, Paul McCartney and John Lennon both became famous recording artists in their own right. But the world-beating music they collaborated on together as Beatles is considered superior to their solo work. Few stars emerge in a vacuum.

What does this mean for you, especially if you don't belong to a team that has the weekly meetings described by Johnson? Be in the flow of your profession. Spend as much time as you can with a diverse range of client executives and thought leaders in your field of expertise. If you work with a firm, make time to have freewheeling discussions with your colleagues about new approaches to client problems.

Cultivate friends and colleagues who are different from you. I've received lots of interesting ideas and perspectives from people who were entirely outside of the business world. Spend a lot of time listening—you might just get the kernel of an idea for your own version of "Blowin' in the Wind" (see sidebar)!

---

Are you listening carefully to others, and using what you learn to improve and augment your own ideas?

---

## 9. Pause, concentrate, and reflect

"I lived in solitude in the country," said Albert Einstein, talking about the sources of his great ideas, "and noticed how the monotony of quiet life stimulates the creative mind." When I lived in London, I had the fortune of knowing bestselling children's author Roald Dahl, who wrote classics such as *Matilda* and *Willy Wonka and the Chocolate Factory.* He had a small shed at the rear of his garden, where, in quiet and solitude, he would do much of his writing.

Something else to consider is that insight often occurs during the letup and relaxation that follows a period of intense activity. Sometimes, ideas come to me during a long shower or a relaxing walk. I quickly write them down in a notebook, and then go back to them later.

If you want to develop more ideas, you simply have to get off the merry-go-round of your daily busyness. I actually think idea generation is like a muscle: you have to practice it on a regular basis. Aim to produce lots of ideas, without prejudging them, and then after a few days or weeks, winnow them down.

---

Do you make time for intentional reflection? How could you set aside more thinking time in your weekly schedule?

---

## 10. Be intellectually eclectic

Eclectic means diverse and wide-ranging. Peter Drucker, who is considered one of the leading management thinkers of the 20th century, epitomized this quality. He developed many concepts that are now an integral part of our business language, such as the knowledge worker and the idea of management by objectives. Drucker himself masterfully combined what the great Renaissance artist Leonardo referred to as "Arte e Scienza" (art and science). He started his career as a journalist and economist. Then, he moved to the United States from Europe and began studying the management of large corporations like General Motors. Then he became a professor and consultant. He was devoted to his many side interests, such as Japanese art.

Good ideas are often developed at the intersection of diverse fields or markets, and/or by outsiders. The most obvious examples are Apple's development of the iTunes music store in 2001 and the iPhone in 2007. In both cases, Apple was an outsider to these industries—cellular handsets and music distribution—and yet they reinvented them.

Your measure of success shouldn't be whether or not you develop an industry-shattering idea for each of your clients. That said, if you do, more power to you—and, please do write a review of this book where you mention that accomplishment. All joking aside, by reading widely and engaging in exploratory learning outside your field of expertise, you are more likely to develop big-picture ideas that your clients will find unique and appealing.

Being eclectic and developing breadth will help your career as well. I've mentioned already that when I was living in London, our firm's CEO was trying to figure out how to revive our Italian business. He quickly determined that there was only one partner in the entire firm who spoke Italian—me. I had studied Italian in Florence, Italy, during my college years. At the time, learning Italian seemed pretty frivolous. When I was then offered the position of country CEO for Italy, I was scared to directly ask my wife, Mary Jane, if she would consider it. So I called her and said, "So . . . how would you like to learn Italian?" She somehow knew what I meant, and exclaimed, simply, "I'm in!"

Are you a narrow expert or a "deep generalist" who has both knowledge depth and breadth?

## Using big-picture thinking with your clients

The question you may be asking right now is this: "My clients know their company and industry much better than I do. How am I supposed to bring them big-picture thinking that they haven't already thought of?" Your job is broader and more nuanced, however, than coming up with your clients' next big idea. It is to push and stretch their thinking about their toughest issues. To give them small ideas that will incrementally improve their business. To share insights based on your in-depth experience. Don't let the best become the enemy of the good. You shouldn't allow the fear that your insights aren't "earth-shattering" keep you from developing and sharing your ideas.

**PUTTING KEY IDEAS INTO ACTION**

1. With each of your clients, get into the habit of climbing a tree (metaphorically!) to see the landscape that surrounds them. Do you understand the total organizational context they work in? Are you aware of the external, competitive, and market pressures they experience? What issues should your client be thinking about that day-to-day operational pressures prevent them from seeing?
2. Remember: For every 10 ideas or suggestions you provide, a given client may ignore or reject five of them, agree to think about three of them

(*continued*)

**PUTTING KEY IDEAS INTO ACTION (*CONT'D*)**

further, and accept and act on just a couple. You need all 10, however, to arrive at the few that are workable.

3. Become what I call a "deep generalist." Continually deepen your expertise in your area of specialization, but also broaden yourself. Many people read or listen to just a few books each year. How about you? Think about a couple of concrete steps you can take this year to expand your general knowledge. This could be through reading, taking a course or workshop, or pursuing a personal interest outside of work.

# Week 12 Get Clients to Root for You

Would you be willing to try out a new plumber or electrician for repairs around your house? If they appeared competent and their prices were reasonable, why not? I'm guessing you would probably be especially open to the idea if they offered something a little different or better than your current supplier.

How about your trusted personal physician or financial advisor? Not so fast. Perhaps, like me, you've been captive on a delayed airplane flight and resorted to perusing one of those in-flight magazines they leave in the seat pocket. And you may have seen the paid advertising section for the "best" doctors in America. Did you immediately think about firing your own doctor and hiring someone in the ad? Probably not.

So what commands your own loyalty? Why is it that certain people are interchangeable, while others feel irreplaceable to you? It's important to understand this dynamic. If you can develop loyal clients who actively root for you—who enthusiastically promote you to others—there's no limit to the growth potential of your business.

## Are you creating personal promoters?

There is a big difference between a satisfied client and a personal promoter. Satisfied clients feel you've met their expectations. You have delivered what you promised. They will likely serve as a reference if asked. They would probably use you again. Or maybe not, if someone else offered to supply the same product or service at a lower cost or with some value-added extras tacked on. It's very important to have satisfied clients. However, a client who is *only* satisfied is not necessarily a *personal promoter.*

It's the difference between a good restaurant and a great one. You rarely tell anyone about a restaurant that's just good. But you can't wait to tell your friends about that amazing new place, with a line outside, that serves the best sushi you've ever eaten . . .

Personal promoters are so enthusiastic about you that they run around their organization encouraging everyone to meet you and use your solutions. They recommend you even when there isn't an exact match between what you do and the apparent need. That's the trust factor at work—it creates a halo around you and the perception of your capabilities. Clients often feel it's better to work with a smart person or firm they trust than take a risk on brand X. They spontaneously give you referrals to friends and contacts in other companies. If they switch jobs, they usually try to bring you in to help.

But there's more. Personal promoters feel you have made a real difference not just to their organization but also to them *personally*. They feel their lives are easier and better because of you. You have made them look good. You've enhanced their careers. They are not just satisfied—they are deeply grateful.

Finally, this type of devoted client feels a strong personal connection to you. You may or may not be friends, but you have gotten to know each other. You've spent time together. You've even been a bit vulnerable with each other. They want you to succeed, and you in turn care deeply about their success.

**THERE ARE NO AGE BARRIERS TO BUILDING PERSONAL PROMOTERS**

I was interviewing a guest CEO at a client conference, and asked her if age was a barrier to becoming her trusted advisor. "No," she emphatically replied. She then told a story about a young woman who was part of her financial advisor's team. Over time, this woman had earned her way into the CEO's inner circle based on hard work and commitment, and by adding value during all their meetings. The CEO even began promoting her services to others. At any age, regardless of where you are in your career, you can build promoters in your clients' organizations. Your foundation is quality delivery. Then, no matter what the age difference, there are always common themes that you can find and connect around.

Over 20 years ago, after leaving Gemini Consulting, I started my own consulting firm. It has grown virtually every year since then, including through several economic downturns. While many things have contributed to my firm's success, developing my fair share of personal promoters has probably been the most important factor. I have ongoing relationships with individual executives that now stretch back decades—in several cases, over 30 years. And I've been working with some of my current clients for well over 15 years.

A global firm I started advising nearly 20 years ago is a good example. Originally, I was brought in by a business unit head to run a one-day workshop for his leadership team. He then asked me to run similar sessions for other executives. Over time, we got to know each other personally. He introduced me to his chief learning officer (CLO), who invited me to develop some programs for other parts of their organization. When we were in the same city together, we typically would meet up for dinner. Before too long, both my original client and the CLO were recommending me to other leaders. I put a team together to help meet this demand, which grew year after year. Later, some of the executives who had attended my programs left to work at other companies. Four of them called me, over a period of several years, creating yet more new clients.

## The loyalty sequence

Engendering client loyalty is not an easy challenge, but neither is it a mysterious process. It requires a devotion to high-quality work and an investment in the relationship-building activities that help cement long-term loyalty. Let's examine the strategies that will help you build your own personal promoters.

There are four steps to developing clients who will enthusiastically root for you. First, deliver high-quality work. Second, build a personal relationship. Third, add personal value that complements the institutional value you've created. And fourth, amplify your relationship. Let's look at why each of these steps is important, and, most importantly, how to execute them.

### 1. Deliver high-quality work

I can't tell you exactly what high-quality work means for you and your clients. But I do know that you can deliver what *you* think is high quality and still not meet your client's expectations. So we're talking about quality and value as perceived by the client.

In advising my own clients, I've been exposed to the work of many other service providers. I've seen great products and services that clients felt were just average. I've also seen what I believed was poor-quality work that the client thought was terrific. So there's more to client perceptions than objective quality.

To ensure your quality is recognized, I suggest you do three things:

1. *Explicitly discuss your client's expectations.* Define, agree, and track the measures of success for your delivery, whether it's a product or a service.
2. *Ensure your client sees the value you are adding.* Don't be shy about tracking benefits and impact, and sharing this information on a regular basis. If you're hesitant to highlight your joint accomplishments, always remember that if things go south, your client won't hesitate to confront you about your shortcomings!
3. *Communicate often.* I had a financial advisor once who was poor at keeping in touch. After a while, I just couldn't see the value he was adding. The relationship became a bit like a black box—I didn't know what he was doing to earn his fees. Don't let that happen to you. Transparency and communication enhance a client's perception of value.

The road to developing a personal promoter starts with quality work that meets your clients' expectations. But it doesn't end there.

## 2. Build a personal relationship

Does building a personal relationship with a client mean you become friends? Not exactly. Occasionally, you *will* become friends with a client. But that's not what I'm talking about here. I mean getting to know your client as a *person*—for example:

- Spending face-time together and talking about things other than business.
- Getting to know each other as people, not just professionals on different sides of a transaction.
- Learning about your client's personal agenda—personal priorities, needs, and goals.
- Discovering things you may have in common, such as personal interests, hobbies, life experiences, and so on.

There are many obvious reasons why it's critical to get to know your client as a person. But here's one you may not have focused on: It is only when we feel a personal connection to someone that we really root for them. As I said earlier, it's a key factor in the difference between the loyalty you feel to a tradesman who does a small repair in your house and your personal physician.

Here are some road-tested strategies to help you build a personal relationship with your key clients:

1. *Follow your client's lead.* Move slowly and take small steps. Some clients like to spend time getting acquainted on a personal level before doing business. Others like to get right down to the business at hand and skip the small talk. If someone is very private, *gradually* build familiarity.
2. *Be intensely curious.* Take a keen interest in other people and their lives. Ask questions about their interests, experiences, families, aspirations, vacations, opinions, and so on.

3. *Cultivate your own interests.* Make time for hobbies and other interests outside of work. Read widely. As the CEO of one of my clients said to me, "How can you be interesting to others if you have no interests?"
4. *Practice appropriate self-disclosure.* You have to be willing to talk about yourself and reveal things about your own life if you expect clients to open up to you (just don't talk *too* much or get *too* personal, too soon!).
5. *Look for similarities and commonalities, and use them to connect.* Engage with clients around common interests and experiences, mutual acquaintances, life's concerns and challenges, family, and so on. Search for what you have in common, not how you are different.
6. *Invest in face-time to build familiarity.* Particularly at the beginning of a relationship, it's important to build up a reservoir of face-to-face interactions. Familiarity leads to likeability and trust.
7. *Be human and accessible.* Show confidence tempered by humility ("I'm confident this is the right step for you. It's worked well with other clients. But only you can decide if it's right . . . "). If appropriate, admit that you may have been wrong about something or someone.
8. *Ask for advice.* People like to help others and they feel good about doing so. Advice could be both professional—e.g., asking a client's input on an article you have drafted—and even personal, if you already know each other pretty well.
9. *Look for "breakthrough" moments.* What will be a real test of fire, a crucible, for your client? An upcoming board meeting? An executive offsite? A major speech? A corporate reorganization? Be there for the big moment. Invest to support your client. A conflict or a crisis, if handled properly, can lift the relationship to the next level.
10. *Use humor.* Humor is a universal way of connecting to others and diffusing tensions. Make fun of the crazy

situations you find yourselves in. Make fun of your own foibles, and of human nature in general.

11. *Change the "relationship environment."* Get out of the office, even if it's to a coffee shop down the street. A different physical environment will change the quality and tenor of your interactions. People open up more when they get out of the office, and they talk about things other than business.

### *Pitfalls of getting personal*

There are a few pitfalls to watch out for as you try to get to know your client as a person. First, don't overdo it and make your client feel uncomfortable. As one British executive told me, "Don't get too 'mate-y' with me at the beginning of a relationship."

Second, don't overreach. Unless there is clear personal chemistry, be careful about trying to socialize with someone who lives in a very different world than you. One of my clients was a senior partner in a major professional firm. Many years ago he led a large consulting project for GE, when the legendary Jack Welch was still CEO. He made a presentation to a small group of executives, which included Welch. Afterward, my client said to him, "Why don't we have dinner together some time?" Welch apparently responded, with a sharp edge to his voice, "Frankly, I've got better things to do with my time than have dinner with you." Ouch.

Third, never get so close to a client that you lose your objectivity. In my case I often do get to know my clients quite well. If I become friends with them, however, it's often when I am no longer advising them directly or working with their organization at all.

Finally, don't confuse "schmoozing" or socializing with adding value in the relationship. They are related—the better you get to know your client, the more value you can add. But don't think you can buy love. Most anyone can procure concert tickets for a client, but only a few can consistently add value to their most important challenges.

### 3. Add personal value

Your contract with a client nearly always specifies the *institutional* value that you will deliver. To create a true personal promoter, however, you have to also add *personal* value. Here are seven ways you can do this. I've framed them as questions.

Think about an important, individual client you work with. How often have you done the following things?

1. *Crisis.* Have you gone above and beyond to help them during a crisis or especially challenging time? For example: made yourself available at odd hours, invested extra time to give advice and support, or worked with them to formulate short-term action plans.
2. *Career.* Have you helped them become better executives and leaders? For example: given them ideas and suggested opportunities to enrich their careers or provided coaching on achieving their performance goals and demonstrating their leadership capabilities.
3. *Learning.* Have you contributed to their learning and helped sharpen their knowledge and skills? For example: given them curated articles and books that align with key interests or provided significant learning experiences through firm events, activities, or conferences.
4. *Team Management.* Have you advised your client on how to develop, lead, and get the most out of his or her team? For example: shared observations about the team's development needs, described the gap between where they are today and where they need to be, and made recommendations for improvement.

5. *Network.* Have you added "network value" by connecting them to valuable, relevant contacts (yours or your firm's)? For example: introduced them to a peer at another company who is facing similar challenges or who was also recently promoted to the same role.
6. *Family.* Has there been an opportunity to help them with family-related challenges and interests? For example: given advice to a child on careers or college admission, helped a newly relocated family find appropriate community resources, or advised a family member or friend on getting summer or full-time employment.
7. *Community and Non-profit.* Have you taken an interest in and helped facilitate their community and non-profit interests? For example: donated to their favorite non-profit cause, introduced them to someone who could help them get involved in the leadership or board of a non-profit organization, or connected them to community leaders and causes.

### 4. Amplify your relationship

A final strategy to get clients to vouch for you is to *ask.* There's evidence that when people give you a public endorsement, their positive opinion about you is strengthened. When clients give a public testimony, in short, they are more likely to subsequently defend their enthusiasm for you and your work. For a similar reason, when we share a goal or commitment out loud in front of others, it's more likely we will accomplish it. It increases our commitment to execution.

You should routinely ask your best clients for referrals. One of the companies I advise recently surveyed their own clients and asked the question: "Would you be willing to give us a referral to a friend or colleague?"

About 50% said yes. How many of those do you think my client had ever *asked* for a referral? Not very many. If a client is satisfied with your work and feels a strong personal connection to you, they generally will be happy to give you a referral or a testimonial. But often, you have to ask. If you and your company are successful, it may not even occur to your clients that you actually want or need more business!

Referrals can be more successful when you make a specific request. It's fine to ask the general question, "Do you know anyone in your network who could benefit from the kinds of solutions and services we offer?" I think it is more effective, however, to identify someone in your client's orbit whom you would like to meet. Do some research about people your client knows. Then say, "I understand you know Elizabeth Garcia at Consolidated Industries. We've done a lot of great work in their industry, and they are exactly the kind of client who really benefits from our solutions. Would you be amenable to making an introduction for me?"

Another way to amplify your relationships and create "rooting" opportunities is to form client events and communities. For 10 years I ran, together with the former CEO of my old firm, a forum for senior executives on developing and growing client relationships. At times we had up to 15 top executives in the group. It was called the Client Leadership Forum, and it met twice a year. There was, above all, high inherent value for the participating executives, who actively shared best practices and common challenges. But in addition, they often enthused to each other about their experiences working with me and my colleague, James Kelly. The forum dramatically reinforced their already-positive views. Even a small breakfast or dinner event can achieve this effect.

## PUTTING KEY IDEAS INTO ACTION

1. To build an authentic connection with others, you need to be willing to share about yourself. Concepts like "self-disclosure" and "vulnerability" may sound scary, but there's solid research that shows they enhance your likability and help the other person open up. I wouldn't suggest you wear your heart on your sleeve or share long stories about your most abject failures, but you *do* want to come across as human. People who come across as perfect or project invulnerability can seem cold and aloof.
2. Start with the relationships you currently have. Is there a client you've been working with for some time you don't know very well? What next steps could you take to learn more about him or her as a person? Sometimes the simplest questions can invite a rich conversation, such as "So how did you get your start in this business?" or "Where did you grow up, and what was it like for you?"

# Week 13 Build Senior Executive Relationships

Have you ever invested time with a client to develop a proposal that was just perfect for their needs? But it turned out his boss had something very different in mind, and the proposal you sweated over died on arrival? Your client, eyes averted, may have apologetically murmured something like, "Turns out our senior vice president has decided to go in a different direction."

This happened to me a handful of times early in my career. I remember one incident that really stung. I spent months wooing a prospective client. I shared all kinds of ideas with her, adding value in multiple ways. I wrote a blockbuster proposal. She kept telling me it was "essentially" her decision to make. We set a kickoff date for the project. Then both shoes dropped. Her boss's boss announced a change in strategy. The work, which I confidently assumed was sold, got shelved.

So I vowed to become the guy the senior vice president would call for help—not the person the middle manager gave the bad news to. Over the ensuing years I intentionally cultivated relationships with senior decision-makers. They became the growth engine of my business and a firewall that protected it during economic downturns.

You should aspire to build relationships with senior executives who are decision-makers for many reasons. C-suite executives and other top leaders can create a budget where there was none. They are focused on revenues and profits, not just costs, so they'll readily see the value in a larger, high-impact proposal. These leaders make decisions about strategy and policy, which you need to understand in order to put your offerings in a bigger context. They can unblock a sale that is stuck. Often, they are the ones who have to approve large contracts.

**PHYSICIAN, HEAL THYSELF**

*(WE ALL MESS UP)*

When I published my second book, it had been over 20 years since I had earned my MBA at Dartmouth's Tuck School. A bit impetuously, I decided to send a copy of it to all my classmates.

A few days later, my phone rang. It was William. I hadn't spoken to him since graduation. All I could remember was that he had taken a sales job with a company in New York. He said he had received my book, *Making Rain*, and really liked it. "So how's it going there?" was all I could ask, blithely ignorant of what had transpired over the last two decades.

"Good," William replied.

"What are you up to?" I tentatively inquired. "Still in sales?"

"I'm the CEO," he answered. This was a $12 billion company!

"Gee, that's nice" was my idiotic response.

He became a client, but it was a rough start that morning!

Another less obvious but compelling reason you should get to know senior executives is that they can recommend you to other important decision-makers. The executive suite is a bit like an exclusive club. Just knowing one member is often sufficient to qualify for membership.

Top executives are often not the direct buyers of your services. But you still want to know them and have them on your side. Most of my multi-year, seven-figure client relationships have had either the sponsorship or direct sanction of a powerful executive.

Building relationships with senior executives, however, is probably the single most vexing challenge for my clients. Why? Because it's hard. These individuals are besieged daily by people who want to sell them something, influence them, or obtain a favor. They're not easy to reach. (Maybe that's why good political lobbyists, who can get in front of top politicians, make so much money!) When you do get a meeting, you have to be quick on your feet, flexible in your approach, bold in your positions, and willing to take risks. Then you have to build an ongoing relationship—which is actually much harder than getting the first meeting.

So this week, I'm going to share a set of proven strategies that will help you move up and connect with important decision-makers.

## Gaining access to the C-suite

I have successfully followed four main strategies for gaining access to senior executives. My clients have also used these to great effect. The first three take time to develop, but if you're successful, they will create momentum that lasts for years. The fourth strategy, moving up with current clients, can achieve rapid results.

### 1. Follow the person not the position

I met one of my longest-standing clients when he was a director at a bank. I was only 28, and he was 40. I wasn't his trusted advisor—my boss, who was the CEO of my old firm, was. But I did good work on the project and we got to know each other. As each of us moved around, I stayed in touch. He periodically made introductions for me to other clients, and was also very supportive of my research and writing when I started my own firm. He eventually became CEO of the bank where he worked, and later, a top executive in the global financial institution that acquired his company. Eventually, over the course of some 30 years, he became CEO or chairman of two major organizations.

Many of the top executives I know today, in short, were not CEOs or business unit heads when I first met them. But I continued to develop these relationships—staying in touch, adding value around an issue of interest, and always—always—doing a high-quality job on any work they sent my way. So this first strategy is to *follow the person, not the position.*

One of my clients became the general counsel of a Fortune 50 company. She said that when she was the deputy general counsel, all the big law firms and accounting firms paid her little attention. They focused their efforts on building a relationship with the general counsel, to whom she reported. They always invited him to the annual golf outings they sponsored and lavished him with attention. When the news of her promotion hit the media, however, her office was flooded with calls from these same firms, all wanting to now do business with her. Her response? She asked each of them, "Where were you five years ago?" Ouch!

Right now, I bet you know lots of people who are in the early stages of their careers. Some of them will become senior executives or even CEOs of significant enterprises. If you've done your job, you won't just have access to them when they rise up—you'll be like old friends because you've known each other for years.

Follow the person not the position. Cultivate relationships with smart, ambitious, interesting people. Follow them throughout their careers. Before you know it, you'll have trusted relationships with key decision-makers. A corollary is this: Invest in and develop your relationships *before* you need them. Otherwise, it's like showing up at your local bank branch and trying to withdraw cash, even though there is a zero balance in your account.

## 2. Become really good at what you do

After playing a lot of tennis one summer, I developed excruciating tendinitis in my right arm. For over a year, nothing alleviated it. Finally, I consulted several local orthopedists in Santa Fe, New Mexico, where we lived at the time. They both suggested surgery. When I asked them, however, how many procedures of this type they had done, the answers varied between five and 12—not nearly enough to be truly skilled at this particular operation. After extensive research, I finally found a well-known hand surgeon in San Francisco who had deep experience in treating my condition. It turned out I had literally torn my extensor tendon off the bone. Fast forward: Two weeks after the surgery my pain had completely disappeared, and today, my right arm is as good as new. The surgeon, Dr. Glen Pfeffer, did an extraordinary job.

The point is that people like you and me go to great lengths to find the right professionals for mission-critical services such as medicine or accounting. So you can imagine how much more a CEO, with vast resources, a peer network, and staff support, can and will seek out those who are outstanding in their fields of expertise.

Do you want to achieve the professional recognition that appeals to senior executives? The first step is to be truly excellent at what you do. I'm sure you know this already—you don't need me to share this truth with you. But intellectual insight doesn't always translate into effective implementation. Nobody gets really good at anything in just a couple of years. Nor can you excel at something if you're a dilettante.

Why do I even mention this? Because our popular culture constantly tries to sell us the "you-can-succeed-in-30-days" gospel. "Speak French in three weeks" trumpets the ad for a language program. "Start earning $10,000 a month in just three months!" shouts a YouTube video on how to "monetize" your expertise. This deceptive, instant-success narrative infiltrates our subconscious. By the way, I speak four languages with varying degrees of fluency, and no, you can't learn French in three weeks by listening to a podcast!

A sales head, for example, told me that she hired a recent graduate for her team. She sat him down and told him she was giving him a major account to manage—a huge opportunity for someone with little experience. His reaction? He responded: "Well, actually, I'd like to do your job, and supervise multiple accounts." No joke. I've heard many similar stories. Every generation has its share of people who put the cart before the horse. Just don't be one of them.

How do you know you're really good at what you do and have the recognition you need to attract experienced client executives into your orbit? Here are some signs you should look for:

- You are able to build and sustain healthy relationships with clients who enthusiastically give you referrals and testimonials.
- You can demonstrate private (e.g., a referral) and/or public (e.g., a written testimonial) endorsements of your professionalism and client results.
- Your business is consistently growing.
- The portion of your business that comes from unsolicited, inbound leads is growing over time.
- If people search your name online before they meet you, they get multiple hits. Their search indicates

things such as: you write and publish, speak on your expertise, are involved with professional or non-profit organizations, have been interviewed by the media and other thought leaders in your field, and so on.

- When you blog, post on LinkedIn, and so forth, you get a sizable number of people viewing/reading your material.
- When a journalist researches a story that touches on your area of expertise, your name comes up as an expert.

No one expects you to check off all of these items after working at your first job for a year. But if you are 10 or 15 years into your career, you ought to be able to say "yes" to many of them.

### 3. Think like a top executive

If you want to develop relationships with C-suite and other senior executives, you have to think like they do. You must develop a strategic mindset (see Week 11 on big-picture thinking), take an enterprise-wide view of client problems (see Week 8 on reframing), and become a "deep generalist"—someone who combines a deep, core specialty with broad-based business knowledge.

I'll be more specific. You have to elevate the level of your thinking and your perspectives when you go to meet with a senior executive. This means you should:

- Focus on how your solutions can impact the big, evergreen issues that are always important to leaders, for example: talent acquisition and development, creating new business models to deal with disruptive technologies, revenue and profit growth, innovation, culture, cost control, and risk management. Any insights or ideas that address these challenges will usually engage their interest.

- Talk about positive return on investment and how your services have helped other clients with the same challenge. Just don't go too deep into the detailed methodologies you will employ.
- Highlight the broad-based impact your approach will have on their organization. Telling top executives who command a $50 million budget that you can save them $75,000 isn't exactly going to grab their attention. The chief human resources officer of a large corporation recently told me, "To get on my calendar and engage me, you need to be talking about something that will affect large numbers of our employees."

Many years ago (I wouldn't do it today!) a friend took me shark fishing on his boat. To catch the sharks, we first used small bait to catch medium-sized fish. We then used those fish to attract the sharks—it's called chumming. To actually capture the shark, we then used a huge chunk of fish on a massive hook.

You don't catch sharks with a small hook and a worm. Similarly, if you want your writing and speaking to attract the attention of leadership, choose big topics that will align with the big challenges they face.

### 4. Move up in the organization

One of the best and most direct ways to build C-suite relationships is to move up in your client's organization. After all, access to them will be easier than with prospects who don't know you. And they will be more inclined to listen to what you have to say since you are already on board.

So with your existing clients, always strive to build relationships with the senior decision-makers. Be very cautious, however, about going over the head of your day-to-day clients. If you do that, you'll undermine or ruin your relationship with them. Going around a mid-level manager looks like a good strategy on paper, but in practice it often backfires. First, you may destroy the trust that person has in you. Second, the senior executive is going to think, "Why aren't they doing this through my team—through the people they are working with day-to-day?" It's a red flag. From the executive's point of view, if you had a great relationship with their people, wouldn't those individuals endorse the introduction?

There are three key moments when you can move up and connect with the top executives at your client:

1. *During the sales process.* Always ask to meet the sponsoring executives in whose area the work falls. Insist, as well, on meeting the economic buyer or decision-maker who will approve the hiring decision. Try to define the total problem and total solution, which will elevate the importance of what you're doing. Finally, connect your proposal to senior management's overall corporate agenda.
2. *During project startup.* With your client, discuss the need to gain the perspectives of key senior executives as you launch the engagement. Explain that your "best practice" is to conduct interviews with senior management as part of your project or contract kickoff. Agree, together, who the key stakeholders should be for your initiative, and create formal touchpoints with them during the project.
3. *During delivery.* As you execute on the commitments in your contract, reinforce the need to gain the perspective and buy-in of key senior executives. Use your time onsite with the client to network, walk the halls, and meet other executives. And always seek opportunities to share the work you're doing with other parts of the organization, e.g., at key company events like planning conferences, offsites, and executive meetings.

## Add value for time

Mid-level managers seek *value for money* when it comes to hiring external providers. In contrast, senior executives are focused first on *value for time.* Sure, they also want value for money. But you will never successfully build relationships with them if you don't add value for time in your meetings.

Think about it: Most top executives could fill their days three times over with people who want to meet with them. Why should they make time for you? There must be a compelling reason for them to spend part of their hyper-busy day with you.

If you want to be invited back for a second, third, or tenth meeting, you have to be seen as someone who adds value on the fly, as the conversation progresses.

### Nine ways to add value for time in your executive meetings

*First, start by aligning to their agenda.* Many top executives have told me some version of the following:

> You may have a great product or a wonderful idea, but don't forget that for the near future I am committed to achieving several key priorities for my company. I'm locked into those, through our planning and budgeting process. If you're not talking about how to help me with those, frankly, you won't get my attention.

What are your client's three to five most important priorities, needs, or goals right now? If what you have to say doesn't connect to this agenda, you'll be pushing water uphill.

Also try to understand what's important *right now.* Short-term pressures and events often hijack executives' long-term agenda. Don't be so singularly focused on their highest-level, long-term goals that you miss an opportunity to help them with something urgent, this week.

*Second, provide insight about the external world.* Are you offering valuable information and perspectives about trends, customers, markets, competitors, how other clients are using your solutions to get results, the economy, or government policies?

*Third, provide insight about the internal organization.* Can you enlarge your clients' perspectives based on an intimate familiarity with their organization and people? Are you able to say, "We've been working with your people now for over six months, and we'd like to share some ideas for addressing several important challenges that you face"?

*Fourth, have a strong point of view.* Senior executives respect and are drawn to professionals who have a point of view and a well-thought-out perspective on the issues. Blandness is not memorable. Be willing to take a stand, perhaps a contrarian one. Of course you won't always be right—no one is. But that fact will be less important than demonstrating thoughtfulness, conviction, and raising important issues for discussion.

*Fifth, like a great song, have an opening hook.* You only have a few minutes to grab their attention and get them interested in continuing the dialogue. Think of the Rolling Stones' "Satisfaction" that starts with Keith Richard's thumping guitar riff or Diana Ross and the Supremes shouting, "Stop, in the name of love" to open that iconic song. The intro hooks in these songs command you to listen.

*Sixth, can you frame the issue differently?* (See Week 8 for how to do this.) A big part of leadership is identifying the critical-few issues the organization needs to focus on, and then defining them properly.

*Seventh, be willing to say "no" and challenge them.* In the words of one CEO I interviewed, "Internally, it's hard to find trusted advisors who will really challenge me." Be seen as someone who is, occasionally, willing to say *no* even when it's in your financial interest to say "yes."

*Eighth, show them that you use their time effectively.* Don't confuse quantity of time with quality. If you can help them get more out of their day, or finish a conversation in 45 minutes that others take an hour for, you'll make an impression.

*Finally, add value in different dimensions, large and small.* Do you have a new idea for tackling an old problem? Can you suggest a valuable introduction to expand their network? Can you help on a personal level in some way? How about suggesting ways for their team to be more effective? Could you offer to review a plan or proposal for them?

Adding value for time is the secret to building an ongoing relationship with C-suite executives. It leaves them wanting more. They will walk away from a discussion with you thinking, "That was a good conversation. I learned something. I'd like to meet again."

## Developing an ongoing relationship

Once you have established contact, you need to be intentional about building the relationship. Under normal circumstances you won't get many chances to meet with a senior executive. You have to create opportunities for follow-up.

For an existing client, you should try to build in an ongoing meeting process. The trick is to make those conversations engaging, stimulating, and original—otherwise, the executive will delegate his attendance to a subordinate.

One of my clients was a senior audit partner for large, Fortune 100 companies. Upon starting a new engagement, he would tell the CFO, "I'd like to have lunch with you twice a month." Invariably, the CFO would say, "No thanks, it's really not necessary to see you that often." My client would insist, however, and say, "Let's try it for a few months, and if you don't find our discussions valuable, we'll meet less often." He told me his firm carefully prepared for the sessions and added a lot of value in them. Within just a month or two, the CFO would usually be delighted with the lunch meetings and would commit to making them a regular event.

Every relationship is somewhat different. Here are some tips for following up with your senior clients over time:

- Above all, make sure you understand your clients' agenda of major priorities and goals for the year, so that you can stay in touch in ways that are meaningful to them.
- Sometimes, you can identify a very specific issue of great interest to the client. Develop and share points of view, assemble curated research, and identify best practices around that issue.
- Send the occasional, well-chosen article or book (perhaps a piece that you have written) and explain, in just one or two lines, why it is relevant to them and what they may learn from it.
- Offer to make an introduction to another senior-level client of yours.
- Interview them as part of a research program or article you're writing.
- If it's an existing client, try to get him or her involved in the initiatives you are working on for the organization. For example, for one project I asked if I could interview my client's CEO about his experiences and videotape the session. I then used excerpts from the videos during workshops I led for his executives.
- With a current client, become comfortable sharing your ongoing observations about the progress of your

work and additional improvement opportunities you see—they don't have to be "big" ideas. Ideally, get a face-to-face meeting—perhaps over coffee, which is less onerous than lunch or dinner. If you can't see someone in person, send a short, pithy letter.
- Invite senior people to exclusive firm events where they will be mixing with other executives at their level.

Even though many top executives will not directly buy your solutions, it is important to cultivate these relationships. They will help drive the growth of your business, amplify your influence, and increase your impact.

### Play to win, not to not lose

Above all, remember this: When you meet with a senior executive, you must *play to win, not to not lose*. If you play it safe and bend over backwards not to make a mistake or displease the client, you'll be unmemorable. You have to play to win. This means being confident, projecting strong points of view, adding value, asking thought-provoking questions, challenging the status quo, and not being afraid to disagree or gently push back.

Next, in Week 14, I'm going to share one further strategy to help you get connected in the C-suite: *Become a person of interest.*

**PUTTING KEY IDEAS INTO ACTION**

Your most important next step is to choose two or three executive relationships you'd like to develop, and build a plan for each of them. Your starting point has to be a solid understanding of their three to five most critical priorities, needs, or goals.

To help you stay on track, here's a reminder of the 11 most common mistakes I see people make when they meet with senior executives:

1. The executive involves other, more junior stakeholders prematurely, who then torpedo your efforts because they feel threatened.
2. You try to cover too many agenda items in the meeting (three is usually the maximum).
3. You rely excessively on PowerPoint or other written material and are unable to have an authentic, engaged conversation with the client.
4. You talk too much and the client talks too little.
5. You try to sell in the meeting, as opposed to building rapport, understanding their agenda, adding value, and sparking their curiosity to have another conversation.
6. You ask questions that are tedious for the client because they are too general and clichéd.
7. You do not align the conversation to the client's agenda of key priorities.
8. You take too long to get to the point, and you lose the client's focus and attention.
9. You *tell* (describe statistics about your company, talk about methodologies, etc.) instead of *show* (share short client examples, best practices, etc.).
10. You lack self-confidence and walk in feeling like a subordinate. This is then communicated through the words you use, your body language, and your overall attitude.
11. You are boring and unmemorable. Your client meets with dozens of people every day—you have to stand out.

Week

# 14 Become an Irresistible Person of Interest

Everyone wants to have relationships with executive decision-makers and other important influencers. As I pointed out in Week 13, however, getting on the calendar of the CEO is like snagging a table reservation at the latest, hottest Manhattan restaurant. Without connections or celebrity, it's nearly impossible. I've seen this from the inside, while advising many C-suite executives. There's just endless demand for their time.

Let's do a thought experiment. What if this situation were turned upside-down? What if top executives were actively seeking you out? What if, when you called them for an appointment, they were delighted to hear from you and cleared their schedules to make room for you? How would this feel, and what would it do for your business?

A pipe dream? No. You may not develop quite the renown of star defense attorney Mark Gerargos or decluttering expert Marie Kondo, but you can absolutely increase your gravitational pull. I call it "becoming a person of interest to the C-suite."

Technically, a person of interest—in the US—is someone police want to question because they may have witnessed, have information about, or been involved with a crime. They are being "actively sought out," which is the sense in which I am using it here. For our lexicon, a person of interest is someone whom senior executives are drawn toward. Someone they want to associate with, do business with, and get advice from.

So how do you become a person of interest? First, I'll explain the three main assets that top executives ultimately seek when considering a close relationship with an advisor or service provider. These are *what you know*, *who you know*, and *who you are*. Then, I'll share strategies for developing them.

## What you know

The first factor that attracts top executives is *what you know*. If I am a CEO, and I'm hosting a year-end leadership conference, whom will I pick as a speaker? Someone who advertises himself or herself as a leadership coach but has no significant credentials? Or someone who has advised a handful of prominent companies and written a book on leadership?

Executives look for individuals who are credentialed. Depending on the clients and their own background and tastes, they may look for different types of credentials. For example—they may have written multiple articles or perhaps a book, attracted a blue-chip client list, been personally referred from another top executive the client trusts, earned a degree at a top school, been chosen as a speaker or panelist at an important conference, and so on. Ideally, you should strive for the Level Three recognition I talked about in Week 2 (client recognition plus media/thought leader recognition).

Senior clients look for something broader than just deep expertise, however. Recall that in Day 1 I used the term "deep generalist"—someone who has in-depth expertise *and* knowledge breadth. If I'm a senior executive running a major function or a business unit, I need experts. But I want my real trusted advisors to have more. Often, we call this elusive but powerful quality "business acumen."

Business acumen integrates five important qualities:

1. *Expertise.* As mentioned previously, executives want to know whether you are truly an expert in your field.
2. *Experience.* Your clients need reassurance that you've addressed this same issue many times before, most likely in their specific industry and/or function.
3. *Breadth.* Most senior executives want someone who understands the interrelationships between different parts of their business. Executives have described this to me using phrases like "big-picture thinking," "an enterprise-wide perspective," or "an integrated view of my problems."
4. *Judgment.* Clients face more strategic and operational choices than ever before. You establish yourself as a valuable peer when you demonstrate the ability to evaluate different courses of action and help your clients make tough decisions.
5. *Insight.* Insight means having a strong sense of perception. Advisors with insight are able to see the issues clearly and separate the wheat from the chaff. Insight brings data and information to life and makes it relevant to your client.

## Who you know

Senior executives are often eclectic individuals who like to cultivate relationships with other interesting people. They have very varied networks. You become more interesting to them if you are seen as also having relationships with diverse and noteworthy individuals. I personally enjoy and benefit from knowing a wide variety of people, both within and outside of my profession. Often, I will introduce a client to a relevant contact who can help with an issue or be a useful connection for them. I call this adding "network value."

**DO YOU HAVE THE C-SUITE ATTITUDE?**

A top CEO headhunter told me once about a candidate for a senior job that he turned down after observing him in the reception area of his offices. He said, "The candidate had only been there for a few minutes, and he was sitting quietly on the couch, looking at the floor. That told me right away that he probably didn't have the C-suite mindset—the confidence needed to operate at the level the job required. CEO candidates don't sit and wait—they stand. That way, when you walk in to pick them up and take them back to your office, they are not in an inferior or supplicant position. Most of them do this without even thinking about it. When I walk out and they are standing, the relationship starts on a peer level."

Trivial? Not at all. Clients look at these subtle behavioral clues and make judgments very rapidly.

## Who you are

I have consistently found that senior executives care about the kind of person you are. Your character really matters to them. By *who you are* I mean the ensemble of your behaviors, values, and beliefs—and even your general outlook on life.

Arguably, everyone cares about the values of the people they do business with. A middle manager or a procurement executive obviously doesn't want to deal with someone who lacks integrity. But they will be more tightly focused on your expertise and ability to deliver on a specific task than on your character attributes.

The first step is to exemplify C-suite behaviors. These include confidence, a willingness to challenge, and an action orientation. The latter means focusing on what will actually work versus a clever theory. You must have a peer attitude when you enter the room. Independence is also essential. Can you set aside your own financial or emotional interests and always do what you believe is best for the client—including walking away if warranted?

Second, clients need to respect and feel comfortable with your values and beliefs. This doesn't mean you have to share the exact same ones. The executives you work with do, however, want to know that you stand for something.

These values and beliefs should always include integrity, which is critical to trust. But they go beyond it. There's no tight prescription for what these are—it varies by individual. Some of the following might be included on any executive's list:

- Action bias
- Ambition
- Authenticity
- Caring
- Commitment to a cause or a transcendent purpose
- Loyalty
- Positive outlook
- Relationship orientation
- Risk awareness

You cannot manufacture a set of values and beliefs to match those of your client. But you can be open about what you stand for and what's important to you. You want your clients, in short, to have a clear sense of who you are.

## Strategies to become a person of interest

You can develop *what you know*, *who you know*, and *who you are* through six strategies.

1. **Sharpen your expertise while expanding your knowledge breadth.** A "deep generalist" has a core expertise that is complemented by a broad understanding of the business environment (or government or non-profit world) that clients live in. Deep generalists are able to better position their expertise in the context of the client's overall business, and their breadth helps them make knowledge connections that more narrow professionals cannot see.
2. **Develop your thought leadership—your points of view, insights, and ideas.** If top executives are going to choose an expert, they are unlikely to reach for someone who lives locally and is just "good enough." Instead, they'll find a professional who has a strong reputation in their field.
3. **Be seen as someone who is at the crossroads of the marketplace.** You achieve this by getting out and talking to lots of people in your field and reading widely around your specialty. If clients see you as being in the flow of things—as having the latest information about companies, markets, executive careers, trends, and so on—they will always make time to see you.
4. **Become a person with interests.** Most C-suite executives are passionate about every aspect of their lives—both at work and at home. Over dinner with a senior client, you're more likely to spend time talking about life outside the office than life in it.
5. **Build an eclectic network.** The diversity and strength of your personal network helps shape the

impression you give your clients. Do you know people your C-suite clients would also appreciate knowing? I'm an advocate of working to deepen relationships with 10 to 25 key stakeholders in your career, but don't forget about the concept of "weak links" (see the work of sociologist Mark Granovetter). There is great value in knowing people outside your inner circle who can connect you to other networks.

6. **Develop, manifest, and communicate your core beliefs and values.** Have you ever sat down and tried to define what's really important to you? Both in your professional life and personal life? The first step is to articulate these to yourself. Then you can exemplify them in your day-to-day client work. If *you* don't know what you stand for, then clients won't either.

## Getting even better at what you do

As I write this, I am learning J. S. Bach's gorgeous cantata, "Sleepers Awake," for classical guitar. It looks easy on paper, but for a variety of reasons it's quite hard to learn and play well. If you don't know it, look it up and listen to it. Just playing the piece over and over again, without thinking about what I'm doing, doesn't actually make me much better at it. This helps me memorize, but not improve my performance. Instead, I have to break it down and practice the most difficult sections separately. I also have to concentrate immensely. I silence my cell phone and immerse myself in the music.

I lack a key ingredient, however—feedback. Right now I'm not working with a teacher. For all I know, I'm playing a wrong note over and over again—or using the wrong fingerings. But without an independent observer who gives me feedback, I'll just keep on making the same mistakes.

Sound familiar? Just because you do something repeatedly—such as analyzing a common client problem—doesn't mean you get better at it. How do you know how to improve the effectiveness of your client meetings? You need someone who can give you feedback—either the clients themselves, or perhaps more likely, a colleague who is present.

The way you steadily improve your skills is to use what are called *deliberate practice* techniques. Psychologist K. Anders Ericsson has pioneered the concept of deliberate practice. One of his core ideas is that improvement in a skill is based on the quality and intentionality of your practice, not simply how many times you perform it. If you aren't familiar with this approach, you should really take it to heart and use it. If you already understand what it is, this section will serve as a brief refresher for you.

Here are the core elements of learning through deliberate practice:

**Isolation.** Great performers isolate very specific aspects of what they do and practice them until they are improved. For example, you might rehearse and polish just the opening minute of a speech, to make it more powerful and impactful. A tennis player might practice one element of a serve, such as the ball toss, over and over again.

**Repetition.** Thoughtful, *attentive* repetition is essential to improve each aspect of performance. It's quite common, for example, for a military special operations team to practice a specific mission dozens of times before deploying. I learned this principle from my son, who spent over a decade in special operations and went on many tough combat deployments. He told me: *In battle, you don't rise to the occasion—you sink to the level of your training.* By the way, these special ops units don't just practice. They always conduct what is called an "after-action review." The team meets afterward to carefully assess what went well and what they could have done better. How often do we do that in our work lives?

**Feedback.** Lots of people "practice," some for years and years, but they never improve very much. We need objective feedback from a teacher or coach who can show us what we're doing wrong and how to improve. Otherwise, we embed bad habits in our work. CEO coach and bestselling author Marshall Goldsmith refers to this as "management superstition." Successful people often do some things poorly, but overall do enough things well that they are high achievers. The problem is, they aren't able to distinguish between their strengths and weaknesses. They end up attributing their success to some practices that are ineffective, similar to rubbing a rabbit's foot for good luck!

**Difficulty.** To get better, you need to push yourself and tackle ever-more-challenging levels of performance. I use an online training program called BrainHQ, which is a kind of mental gym to sharpen your core cognitive skills. It's based on leading-edge neuroscience. One of the characteristics of the program is that as you improve at an exercise, it automatically gets more and more difficult until you feel like you're failing. Only when taxed in this way does your brain begin to build new neural connections and capabilities. At work, if you don't push yourself by taking on difficult tasks, you won't build new levels of skill.

**Concentration and Focus.** To improve you must focus your undivided attention on the task you are practicing. Forget the fake glamour surrounding the ability to "multitask." It's bunk—multitasking is inefficient and a terrible use of your brain. High-quality work and creative ideas usually emerge from intense concentration and long periods of reflection.

**Metacognition.** Have you ever seen colleagues make a presentation and fail to pick up cues from their audience across the table? Instead of responding to the signals they're getting, they go on and on, like an automated player piano that has no "off" switch! So the final skill required for mastery of anything is called *metacognition.* High achievers, while they are in the midst of actually performing, are able to observe themselves and what's going on around them, and make adjustments to their behavior and tactics. This requires awareness, self-confidence, gravitas, and a high level of comfort in your craft.

Use these ideas, and you, too, will develop into a person of interest. If you think you're *already* pretty interesting to top executives, congratulations. But don't let it go to your head—I wager you can still get better.

**PUTTING KEY IDEAS INTO ACTION**

Start by assessing the degree to which you are currently a *person of interest* to clients. How would you rate yourself, on a scale of 1 to 5 (1 = very weak and 5 = very strong) on each of the person-of-interest dimensions? (*Note:* I include a more structured person-of-interest assessment in my *Client Growth Workbook,* which you can download for free at andrewsobel.com/growth-workbook.)

### What You Know

- Branded expertise
- Business acumen

### Who You Know

- A rich, diverse network

### Who You Are

- C-suite behaviors
- Values and beliefs

Next, pick two or three things you can do, this year, to be more of a person of interest to clients. For example, could you:

- Engage in activities that will improve your recognition and strengthen your brand?
- Work on building a more varied and diverse personal network?
- Pick a skill or behavior and improve it through deliberate practice—including getting objective feedback about your performance from someone you trust?
- Cultivate a personal passion or interest outside of work?

# Day 100 Keep Your Clients for Life

## The beauty of staying in touch

A few years ago, I received a phone call from an old client of mine. It had been five years since we had worked together. We had periodically been in touch, but there was never a compelling reason to reengage. The reason for the call? He had just read my newsletter, *Client Loyalty*, and wanted to discuss a project. My article that month happened to be about an urgent challenge his firm faced.

It turned out that during those five years, he had always read the subject lines for my newsletter emails. Once in a while, when one piqued his interest, he opened the email and read it. Now, finally, the stars had aligned. My chosen topic that month, and the value I provided in the article, matched an important need of his.

I used to be preoccupied with the sad fact that for years, some clients seemed to pay no attention to my newsletter. But after many incidents like this one, where someone would contact me after a long period of silence, I realized something very powerful was at work.

I call it the "radar screen theory of selling." You need to stay on your clients' radar screen. You have to be top of mind when they have a need in your area of expertise. Or, as one of my clients once told me, "You have to be there when the dam breaks."

So stay connected, with both current and past clients, in meaningful ways. Keep your ideas—your value—in front of them on a regular basis. It's essential if you want to keep clients for the long term.

## Treating old clients like brand new ones

When I interview senior executives about the times when they have switched providers, they consistently say things like this about the incumbent:

- "They got complacent and took our business for granted."
- "They stopped trying hard. Lately, they haven't been very responsive."
- "Some of the other firms calling on us were adding more value—and we aren't even their client!"
- "There were little slipups. And they kept changing out members of the team."

Complacency, which sums up the gist of what these buyers are saying, is the enemy of the successful professional. I have seen it time and time again. If a client relationship isn't improving, it is usually getting worse—except we often don't see the deterioration. While there are major differences between the dynamics of professional versus personal relationships, the destructive power of complacency is a notable similarity. Think about it: marriages and partnerships often break up when one or both parties stop trying. When they stop caring as much as they used to. When they take the other person for granted.

While marriage is a complex topic, I firmly believe that one of the keys to success is treating your spouse or partner as a newlywed. When you're courting someone you think of him or her often. You bring them special presents. You tell them how important they are. You want to look your best for them. You are patient and tolerant. But fast-forward 10 or 20 years and those caring habits can easily fade, replaced by an immersion in daily routines and self-focus.

In short, go to the 100th meeting with your client with the same enthusiasm, new ideas, attention, and desire to make an impact that you displayed in your first conversation. If you do, you'll dramatically increase your odds of retaining them. If you don't act like this, why would they stick with you?

## Get rid of "me"

A "me-centric" attitude doesn't help attract clients into long-term relationships with you. It does enable some people to succeed in the short term, but it's a shallow way to live. There's a better and more powerful approach: "you/we."

Through both my research and my personal experience, I've found there are six personal qualities that, in particular, help fuel trusted client relationships. They enable you to maintain your center of gravity through the inevitable ups and downs of working with clients. They are:

- **Curiosity.** Curiosity drives a thirst to learn about knowledge and other people. It motivates you to ask thoughtful questions. Without curiosity, you won't empathize effectively. A lack of interest in others makes you look self-satisfied or even arrogant.
- **Listening.** Good listening is a rare skill. Good listeners truly hear what their clients are saying. They ask questions and then listen, affirm, synthesize, and act on what they've learned.
- **Generosity.** When you're generous, you demonstrate a readiness to give more than is expected. It's an attractive, winsome quality that increases trust and likability. If trust is the universal lubricant of relationships, generosity is what fuels them.
- **Patience.** The world around us rarely adheres to the schedules we demand. Patience will save you a lot of aggravation and anger, because nothing ever happens as quickly and neatly as we'd like. Think of yourself as a gardener as you work with clients. You need an abundance of patience to commit the time and effort required to grow healthy flowers and vegetables. Two of my best clients today, for example, took a year and three years, respectively, to engage me after our first conversation!
- **Humble Confidence.** Confidence tempered with a good dose of humility is highly attractive to clients. Self-importance, in contrast, is terribly distasteful. The author C.S. Lewis described it this way, referring to what it's like to meet a humble person: "Probably all you will think about him is that he seemed a cheerful, intelligent chap who took a real interest in what you said to him . . . . He will not be thinking about humility: he will not be thinking about himself at all."

- **Caring.** Clients want to know whether you care about them and about their business. When you show real concern for their problems, their aspirations, and what they are going through, it puts the relationship on another plane. Without caring, your expertise and solutions are hollow. By themselves, they qualify you for a short-term transaction, but not an enduring relationship.

Many of the ideas in this book are about things you do *with* and *for* clients. But if your core isn't solid, those strategies are a house of cards. Your expertise can only take you so far without curiosity, generosity, patience, deep listening, measured self-confidence, and authentic caring.

How are *you* doing on these attributes?

## The final secret

While researching my first book, *Clients for Life*, I interviewed a large selection of CEOs about their most trusted advisors and service providers. One of these executives was Chuck Lillis, who at the time was the CEO of the cable company MediaOne, which was later sold to ATT for $64 billion.

When I asked Chuck about the qualities he looked for in an external advisor, he said something quite powerful: "I wish all my advisors were independently wealthy."

"Can you say more about that?" I responded.

"Then," he clarified, "I would know that the individual was giving me advice that was completely objective and unbiased by any financial considerations. They would always be candid and have no fear of telling me what I need to hear rather than what they think I want to hear. They would have my best interests in mind at all times."

You may not (yet!) be independently wealthy. But even if you still have to work for a living, you can possess the *mindset of independent wealth*. How so? By *acting* as if you are independently wealthy. If you do, you'll behave in ways that endear clients to you. You'll push back or even say "no" to a client idea or proposal with no concern about the financial consequences. You'll willingly invest in the relationship and take time to learn about your client's business. Professionally, you might be open to try more new things, since you wouldn't be afraid of failure. I also think you would be more inclined to insist on framing the client's problem correctly and charging appropriate fees for your work.

But how do you actually embody this mindset? You can do it by exemplifying three behaviors when you are with your clients:

*First, walk in as a peer.* Treat your client like a colleague or friend, not as a superior. Be polite and courteous, but not deferential or fawning. The first sale is always to yourself. If you don't believe you have something valuable to share with others, they won't believe it either.

*Second, ignore the clock.* In a world of unlimited distractions and preoccupations, be totally and completely immersed in the conversation. Listen at the highest level of concentration possible. Don't check your smartphone, think about your next appointment, or worry about that troublesome email you just spied from your boss or another client. For those 30 or 60 minutes, make your client feel like he or she is the *only* person in your world.

*Finally, exude enthusiasm.* If you're not passionate about your work and thrilled about what you can do for your clients, why would they be? Enthusiasm is an underrated quality. It comes from the Greek *enthousiasmos*, and means a feeling of excitement or fervor. Originally it was used to describe religious passion. In a similar vein, you should demonstrate a zeal for your work. If you're excited about your topic, it will ignite the other person's interest as well. You'll raise the energy level in the room.

* * *

You've now got solutions for overcoming many of your biggest client development challenges—the 14 weeks of this book. Feel free to contact me at andrew@andrewsobel.com with questions, comments, or client success stories—I'd love to hear from you. And, if you want a set of additional resources to help you apply these strategies, you can download my *Client Growth Guide* for free at www.andrewsobel.com/growth-guide.

Here's to your success with clients!

# About the Author

Andrew Sobel is the leading authority on the strategies and skills required to earn lifelong client loyalty and build trusted business partnerships. He is the most widely published author in the world on this topic, having written nine acclaimed books on developing the relationships that matter—with your clients and for your career. In addition to *It Starts with Clients*, these include the international bestsellers *Power Questions* and *Clients for Life* as well as *Power Relationships*, *All for One,* and *Making Rain.* His books have been translated into 21 languages. He has also published over 400 articles and contributed chapters to four books on leadership, strategy, and marketing.

Andrew's unique relationship-building and revenue growth strategies have been codified into both live training and an engaging series of popular online courses available at Learning.AndrewSobel.com.

Andrew has worked for more than 35 years as both a strategy advisor to senior management and an executive educator and coach. His firm has attracted over 150 leading, global companies as clients. These include established public corporations such as Citigroup, Cognizant, and Bank of America, as well as many privately held professional services firms such as Booz Allen Hamilton, PwC, Bain, and Grant Thornton.

His articles and work have been featured in a variety of publications including *USA Today*, *The New York Times*, *BusinessWeek*, the *Harvard Business Review, Forbes,* and *strategy+business*, and he has appeared on numerous national television programs.

Andrew spent the first 15 years of his career with Gemini Consulting (formerly the MAC Group), where he became a senior vice president and country CEO. He lived and worked in Europe for 13 years and speaks four languages. He graduated from Middlebury College with honors and earned his MBA from Dartmouth's Tuck School. He is founder and CEO of Andrew Sobel Advisors, a global consulting and training firm. He can be reached at www.andrewsobel.com.